Poems From My Heart

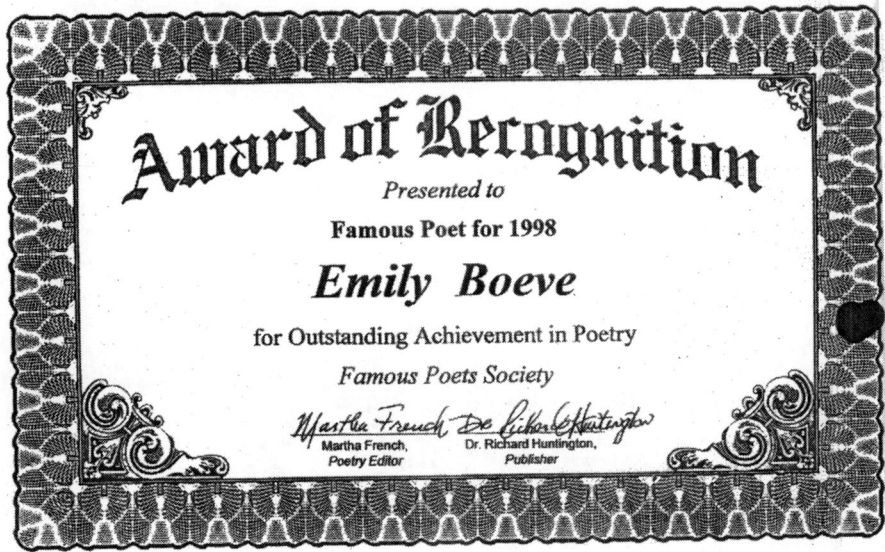

Poems From My Heart

Emily Gaye Boeve

Copyright © 2010 by Emily Gaye Boeve.

Library of Congress Control Number: 2010905318
ISBN: Softcover   978-1-4500-8460-4

All rights reserved. No part of this book may be reproduced or transmitted in any form or by any means, electronic or mechanical, including photocopying, recording, or by any information storage and retrieval system, without permission in writing from the copyright owner.

Composed By: Emily Gaye Boeve

Illustrations By: Leo S. Plato and
                  Emily G. Boeve

First Printing: 1978

Second Edition: 2010

Copyright: 1978, 2009

This book was printed in the United States of America.

To order additional copies of this book, contact:
Xlibris Corporation
1-888-795-4274
www.Xlibris.com
Orders@Xlibris.com
79081

CONTENTS

My Testimony 9
My Testimony of Conversion 10
I Am The Daughter Of The King 12
Being A Christian 13
I Want 14
Only Passing Through 15
Just A Thought 16
Points To Ponder 17
Have You Answered The Call? 18
God's Decision 19
Follow Me 21
My Child My Grace Is Sufficient For Thee 22
My God 24
Look On The Brighter Side 25
My Anger 26
God's Word Is Good 27
Heavenly Crusaders For A Mighty Savior 28
A Floppy Old Hat 29
I Learned It From You 30
Did You? 32
A Prayer 33
My All In All 34
Kneel And Pray 35
As I Recall Thanksgiving 36
Revive 37
Why Wonder? 38
Do Your Father's Work 39
My Prayer 40
Phone Call To A Loved One 41
Hello God 43
I Am . . . . I Am God 44

How I See God	45
Save My Loved One	46
How Much Do I Love Thee?	47
The Little Vessel	48
So Many Words To Choose From	50
Waiting For The Rapture	51
Too Late	52
Voice Of A Sinner	54
And I Was Worried	55
It's Easter	56
Would It Be Enough?	58
Who Cares . . . . Do You?	59
A Plea For God's People	61
Until He Comes	62
Day By Day	63
Share	64
Look Up	65
A Brand New Day	66
Let Me Be More Like You	67
Can This Be Love	68
I Am A Little Church	69
A Prayer From The Ill	70
The Story Of The Samaritan Woman At The Well	71
The Good Samaritan	74
Samaria	75
Leviticus	76
How Strong Is Your Faith? (Book of Job)	77
Moses And The Burning Bush	79
After Thanksgiving . . . What Then?	81
When May I Cry?	82
Thanksgiving	84
Have You Ever Been Lonely	86
On The Other Side	87
What Would Jesus Do?	88
Secure	89
Stain Removal	90
The Virus	91
Teach Me	92
Take My "I"	93

A Special Valentine	94
To A Precious Valentine	95
A Valentine For My Loved Ones	96
A Valentine Wish for Doctors and Nurses	97
What Is A Mother?	98
What The Clay Can Do With The Potter	99
Reality Of Aging	100
I Could Have Been	101
My Baby	102
My Little Boy	103
Heart And Soul	104
I Live To Serve You	105
My Beloved One	106
Dear God, The Trees	107
I Remember Momma	108
It's From Mother	110
Mommy	111
Requiem To Mom	112
A Mothers' Day Prayer	114
Fathers are Special.	115
Dear Daddy	116
Happy Father's Day	118
Come To The Altar	119
Thank You Jesus	120
Thank God	121
A Lump Of Clay	122
Depression	123
Unworthy One	124
To Encourage A Brother	125
Fireside Chat	126
Some People I Remember	127
Reach Out With Loving Arms	128
From The Heart Of A Child	130
Ode To A Prisoner	133
A Church I Dreamed Of	135
Your Best Friend	136
Beggars	137
One Christmas Morn	138
Christmas Time	139

What Do You Want For Christmas?	141
What Does Christmas Mean To Me?	142
The Christmas Tree	143
A New Year's Prayer	144
Promised Land	145
When I Leave This World	146
Genesis One	147
Exodus Chapter 1	149
Exodus Chapter II, Part I	150
Exodus Chapter II, Part II	151
Commit	153
Here I Go	154
Was It Worth It After All?	156
Hello Jesus, Come On In	158
A Loving Farewell	160
Dearly Beloved	161
Departed	162
Soon	163

My Testimony

I searched for years, til' I came to this place.
Where I finally found, a smile for my face.
One night, as I was lying in bed,
A part of a verse, came into my head.
I couldn't sleep, so I arose
And by the Holy Spirit, I was led,
Downstairs to get my Bible.
The twenty third Psalm, is what I read.

Yes, I was looking for Jesus!
I was wandering in fear and full of doubt,
Trying to find Him in churches . . . .
But mostly looking . . . without!
To find my Lord and Savior . . . became my goal.
Then to my surprise, I found Him.
He was right there, all the time,
Just a tuggin' at my soul.

I opened the door and I let Him in.
He lifted all my burdens and He pardoned all my sin.
No longer do I have to search, no longer do I prod.
Now, at last, I've found my Savior,
And I belong to the family of God.
Praise the Lord!
Now, I'm a child in the family of God.

cpwrt. 1978
EMILY BOEVE

My Testimony of Conversion

I was born and baptized as a baby,
into the Catholic religion. At age six,
My parents got a divorce and
I was placed in my aunt and uncle's home.
They were Methodist. At age twelve,
I was sprinkled with water. This was
Their method of baptism.
I didn't know what that meant, but all the children
My age did it. By the ripe old age of sixteen,
the devil had a hold on me and
he didn't let go until I was thirty seven.
This is when I moved back to
Bellevue, Ohio and by the hand of providence,
I was led to Providence Baptist
Church. In 1975, it was necessary for me
to have major surgery.
I went into that
surgery, under conviction. I was lost and scared.
When I had been home for
about a week, my youngest son fell,
while riding his bike and broke his leg.
He was in the hospital for the next month.
A couple of days after he came home
from the hospital,(to spend the next five months
in a body cast), our church
began its fall Revival.
Now, all the time from my surgery, up to that point, I was
under conviction. Then one day, our pastor
and the visiting evangelist came to
visit me. When they came through the front door,
another couple came through
the back door. The devil knew that I couldn't and
wouldn't talk in front of my

other visitors. We made an appointment for the pastor
and the evangelist to come
back the next day. Then the devil really began
to work on me. In my mind, I began
to practice, what I was going to say to them.
This went on for the rest of the day
and far into the night. Finally, I had a blunt talk with God.
I told Him that I was just
going to tell it like it was and if the two men didn't think
I should belong to their
church, then I would look for a church that would accept me,
just the way I was.
The next day, when the men came back,
I told them that I wanted to ask Jesus into
my heart and life and that I wanted to join their church,
but that I had some things
to tell them first, that might mean that
I wouldn't be allowed to join their church. I
then blurted out what I had to say.
The men knelt with me and we three prayed and
I asked Jesus to come into my heart and life and save me.
He did! Now, I can praise
God and thank Him, that now, I'm His child,
for all Eternity. Praise God, I'm a child,
in the family of God!

I Am The Daughter Of The King

I am the daughter of the King.
My Father has given me everything.
He is building me a mansion,
It will be bright and shiny and clean.
T'will be quite the loveliest thing . . .
That I have ever seen.
He has given me a large bright sun,
Perched in a bright blue sky.
A soft green carpet, lies beneath my feet,
With pretty flowers standing by.
Now, I don't need . . . a furry coat,
Or a great big diamond ring.
For I have so much more than that,
Because I am the daughter, of the King.
You wonder why I'm dressed like this,
With no regal robes to wear?
And where's my jewels and crown?
Why, they're at my home, in my Father's loving care.
I find beauty all around me.
Oh, how lucky, I must be.
My Father gave me two good eyes . . .
Just so I might see.
He also gave me two good ears, so I could hear you sing.
And two feet to walk the path . . . He chose . . .
And two hands . . . so I could touch a rose.
He let His only Son, die on Calvary, for my sin.
But when I asked . . . He forgave me . . .
Now I hold Him close within.
He has given me so much, well truly . . . everything!
And I am so very proud to say . . .
I am the daughter, of the King

Being A Christian

To be a Christian . . . Losing logic, is a must.
You just have to follow Jesus . . .
In total faith and trust.
Whatever happens in your life,
Whether good or bad or in between,
Just lean on Jesus and Lean and lean and lean.
We'll know all the answers, when we leave this Earth.
But for now, just trust Him . . . for all you're worth.
When things don't go, the way you think they should . . .
Remember . . . God can take that evil and make it good.
Now it may not be anything you've done . . . .
And don't think for a minute, that the old devil has won.
When things go wrong, keep your eyes on Jesus, that's a must.
Keep looking to Him . . . in total faith and trust.

I Want

I want to follow Jesus, . . . my Lord and my God.
I want to follow the footsteps, that Jesus trod.
To choose my words, with utmost care . . .
Knowing He hears me . . . He's always there.
I want to draw others to Jesus, with kindness and love.
And tell them of Jesus and Heaven and our Father above.
To tell how Jesus died, to save us all from sin,
If we only repent and call on Him.
By His stripes, He will heal, all that is wrong.
Jesus paid it all, like it says in the song.
I want to tell others of Jesus, while I'm still here,
So they'll ask Him in their heart and feel Him near.
They will feel His Love and know no fear.
They'll know forgiveness and feel His love so dear.
Now won't you ask Jesus for forgiveness of your sin,
And open your heart's door and ask Jesus to come in?
If time would end today, you would know such sorrow.
My friend, there's only today, you're not promised, tomorrow.
Won't you ask Jesus to save you now? Please don't wait!
Now is the time . . . Today! Before it's too late!
To make that choice now, would be good and well.
I want you to go to Heaven . . . . not hell.!!!

Only Passing Through

It's such a lovely day,
The sun is shining in a sky of blue.
Slowly, I begin to realize . . . .
That, I too . . . . Am only passing through.

The wind makes a ripple, upon the brook.
It causes the leaves to dance gaily, as onward, I look.
As evening comes, the wind will pass,
And quietly comes the dew.
In my heart, I know, that I too . . . .
Am only passing through.

We face many trials and troubles, in this life.
In many lands, there's hardship and war and strife.
Be of good cheer Christian, I'll tell you what to do.
Bow your head and pray with me . . . .
We're only passing through.

Clouds gather more clouds, as they swiftly pass by.
God expects the same kind of gathering, from you and I.
So witness to many, or just a few, . . . but help them realize.
That we're only passing through.

I'll make a Christian ripple, upon the worldly brook.
I'll wave the Christian banner, as the sinners onward look.
I'll witness to my neighbor and win him to Jesus too,
For now I know, that in this life . . . .
I'm only passing through.

Just A Thought

It's raining Lord . . . .
Thank You Lord, . . . for the rain,
That washes away some of the dirt . . . on the Earth.
But rain can't wash away . . . all the dirt.
Because most of it lies in the hearts and lives of man.
Now, the sun shines brightly . . . .
And dries the drops of rain that have fallen,
Just as Your love shines in our lives . . .
To dry our tears and dispel our troubles.
Thank You . . . Lord . . . for Your love.
And the assurance . . . .
That You are right here with me,
For I need You . . .
And the strength, You have promised . . .
Every minute of every day . . .
Just hold me close . . . . and
Thank You, Lord.

Points To Ponder

Take the "I" out of sin and replace
It with an "O". You'll get the Son,
Who died for our sin.
Take the "I" out of live, replace it
With an "O", you'll get love . . . and
That comes from God and makes
Life worth loving and living.
Have a "God" centered life,
Not an "I" centered life.
Change "My will" to "God's will."
When "U" "R" in God's will and
He calls on "U", "U" will say "I will"!
When "U" will do God's will . . . .
. . . . He will! . . . .

Have You Answered the Call?

What can I do? . . . I'm only one.
As I look around, there's so much to be done.
There are the sick and the hungry . . .
And so many are still lost! . . . .
It all takes money . . . but what is the cost?

How much does it take, to feed the hungry,
Visit the sick and the prisoners . . .
And witness to the lost?
Lord, how much will it take?
How do we figure the cost?

Where do you want me to start?
Please dear Lord, just lay it on my heart.
God, there's so much to do . . . I know this,
But I just can't do it all . . .
But Lord, show me where to start . . .
And how to answer the call.

Show me, sweet Jesus . . . how to do my part,
How to do Your will . . . .
And share with others, the joy, that's in my heart.
There's one more thing folks, I'm asking you all.
How about you? Have you answered the call?

God's Decision

God searched through His women folk,
    until He found just the right one.
Mary, a virgin, was chosen, to give birth to God's ony Son.
Jesus, Mary and Joseph went to Jerusalem, for Passover.
    At that time, Jesus was a boy of twelve.
They lost Him . . . then they found Him . . . in the Temple,
    Into the priests minds . . . He was trying to delve.
Joseph was a carpenter, by trade. Jesus helped him with the work.
Jesus, was a fine, obedient young man, His duty, He did not shirk.
Jesus went to see John, the Baptist, saying . . . "Baptize Me."
    That's when Jesus, was thirty years old
        And He began His ministry.
He went forth proclaiming God's word and His laws, to everyone.
He told them that He was the Messiah and God's only Son.
    The Jewish leaders didn't believe Him . . .
        "Blasphemer!" is what they cried.
They asked Him questions then . . . They had witnesses, who lied.
They took Him to the High Courts . . . their charge, still rings.
    "He's a Blasphemer!" He says, "He's King of Kings!"
They sentenced Him to crucifixion . . . the cruelest form of death.
They humiliated Him, beat Him, then . . . they nailed Him to a cross . . .

To take His very last breath.
They placed Him in a borrowed tomb and sealed it,
no one could get in or out.
They were afraid that His followers would steal His body,
And that would cause some doubt.
Three days later . . . on a Sunday morning . . . so fair . . .
An angel rolled the stone away.
The tomb was empty! Jesus, wasn't there!
He arose from the dead, went to His Father in Heaven . . .
Just like He said He would do.
Jesus was a sinless man, but He took our sin upon Himself!
He died . . . For me and you!
Ask Jesus to forgive your sin, then open your heart's door . . . .
And let Him in.
You'll never be a loser again . . .
With Jesus, you will always win.

Follow Me

There was a Daddy, he got in trouble with the law.
He was arrested, at home, for all of his family to see.
While in prison, his five year old son told him . . . .
"I want to be just like you, Daddy!"
The Daddy said, "No, No, Don't follow me!"
There was a young Mother, she sold her body, for a fee.
One day her little girl dressed up . . .
In her Mommy's make up and clothes.
She said, "Mommy, can I go too?" I look pretty . . . See . . . ?
Her Mommy cried as she said, "No, Honey, don't follow me."
A young man became a doctor, with all good intention.
He wanted to save lives of sick people, you see.
But later he began aborting babies, too many to mention.
His young son said, "Dad, I'll be a doctor too,
With abortion as my specialty.
The doctor said, "No son, I gave that up . . .
Please, don't follow me."
A rich middle aged couple, threw a lot of parties.
They were of . . . "High Society."
They'd have lots of food, drinks, drugs and sex . . . .
All of this for free.
As they were being arrested and taken away . . .
The man heard one of his teenagers say,
"There's still some drinks and drugs and food . . .
let's have ourselves a BIG PARTEE!!"
With tears in his eyes, the father said . . .
"Don't do it kids!! Don't follow me!"
Then Jesus came softly, to each family.
He knocked at their heart's door,
With an ardent plea.
"Please open your heart and ask me in . . .
And then, dear children . . . . turn from your sin,
And follow . . . . Follow Me!"

My Child

My Grace Is Sufficient For Thee

When the world throws a curve, or two or three,
And satan's playing a game with me . . .
I know I'm alright and Jesus loves me,
As I hear Him say, gently to me . . . .
My Child, My grace, is sufficient for thee.
My child, My grace, is sufficient for thee.
I claim this promise, He's given to me,
My child, My grace is sufficient for thee.
I've gone down the road of hard knocks before.
My heart was heavy, with the burdens, I bore.
But I see an end to this worry for me . . .
As I hear Him say gently to me . . . .
My child, My grace is sufficient for thee.
My child, My grace is sufficient for thee.
I claim this promise, He's given to me.
My child My grace, is sufficient for thee.
I took Jesus in my heart, one beautiful day,
Now walking with Him, is "The Only Way!"
He keeps growing dearer and dearer to me . . .
As I hear Him say gently to me . . .
My child, My grace is sufficient for thee.
My child, My grace is sufficient for thee.
I claim this promise, He's given to me . . . .

My child, My grace, is sufficient for thee.
Softly He's calling, calling to you . . .
To open your hearts' door, and let Him come through.
Let Jesus in, let Him have His own way.
You'll be so happy, when you hear Him say . . . .
My child, My grace is sufficient for thee.
My child, My grace is sufficient for thee.
I claim His promise, He's given to me . . . .
My child, My grace, is sufficient for thee.

My God

My God shall supply your every need
I learned this from the Bible, Yes indeed.
My God shall heal anything that's sore,
A broken arm . . . . a broken heart and so much more.
If we love and obey Him and do His will . . . .
He'll calm our seas of life . . . saying . . . .
"Peace . . . Peace . . . Peace be still."
My God, is kind and loving and great,
To many, He gives a spouse . . . . a helpmate.
If you ever feel blue and think there's no one to care?
Lift your heart to my God, . . . He's always there.
We give Him so little . . . He gives us so much.
He gives all . . . with His loving touch.
When you sin . . . your conscience, He'll prod.
When you ask, . . . He'll forgive you.
That's my Father, . . . That's my God!

Look On The Brighter Side

Let's look on the brighter side
From this day on.
The sins we have committed, . . . are forgiven . . .
And now they are gone.
Count your blessings, one by one.
Thank God, the Father, for all He has done.
Don't look so angry, don't look so sad.
God sent us His Son, the only one He had.
He could have kept Him in Heaven, . . .
And sent all of us sinners to hell.
But He chose to let Jesus die for our sin.
So, open your hearts' door and ask Him to come in.
Have you received Jesus into your life, my friend?
Have you committed your life to Him . . .
For a love, that will not end?
Just talk to Jesus, for a little while.
You too will find peace, and a happy smile.
When you receive Jesus, He'll turn the tide, . . .
And then we can look . . . . on the brighter side.

My Anger

Dear Sweet Jesus, Oh Savior Devine,
Please help me with this problem . . . . This anger of mine.
Someone says or does something to me . . .
And my anger, just lets go . . . You see.
Then an argument starts, that I just can't win . . .
My anger . . . I fight back . . . even though I know it's a sin.
I try to turn the other cheek or look the other way . . .
But Lord, it hurts me . . . some of the things they say.
Sweet Jesus, did You ever get angry, when You were on Earth?
Did You ever want to shake someone, for all You're worth?
No, I guess You didn't . . . From what the Bible said . . .
You never said a word . . . .
Even when they put a crown of thorns, upon Your head.
They said You were of the devil . . . and that was a lie!
They didn't even believe You, when they heard You prophesy.
You were so kind and tender hearted and loving to all.
And what did they offer You to drink . . . . but bitter gall?
All these things You suffered, are far greater things, I see,
Than any of these minor things, that seem to bother me.
Help me Jesus, to hold my tongue and turn the other cheek . . .
Hold back my fists and help me look the other way.
Lord, fill me with Your wisdom and love . . .
So I won't lose my temper . . . the way I did yesterday.
Grant me strength, dear Jesus, to do what You would do,
Cause Jesus . . . Sweet, Precious Jesus . . .
I want to be . . . more like You.
Amen

God's Word Is Good

There's something I have to tell you,
And it must be understood,
When our Father in Heaven gives His Word,
His Word is always good.

From the beginning, when He made all things . . .
The Heavens, the Earth, the trees and the sea,
Right down to the animals, fish and fowl . . . .
And Adam and Eve . . . . and you and me.

The Earth became corrupt, God said He would destroy it.
He told Noah to build an ark for the animals.
Some came by seven, some by two,
And Noah and his family, they were fit to go too.

Then, God sent His Son, to live and die for man.
Jesus said, :Father, I'll die,
To forgive them and to save them,"
He said, "I know, I can."

God shows us His mercy, at every turn of the road,
He is always there, to lighten our load.
So, give your heart to Jesus, fill your heart with His love,
And when we die we will join Him,
With our Father in Heaven above.

So, now you know of God's Holy Word,
And how it must be understood,
That when our Father in Heaven, gives His Word,
His Word is always good.

Heavenly Crusaders
For A Mighty Savior

We are soldiers of the cross,
A mighty Savior, we do serve.
We are Heavenly Crusaders,
Spreading God's Holy Word.
Let's put on, the armor of God,
Against the devil, we will stand.
We'll follow our Mighty Savior,
And spread His word, across the land.
Let truth, gird you round about,
With the breastplate of righteousness,
You'll have no fear or doubt.
Lead On! With a mighty shout!
The Gospel of Peace, will shod your feet.
The Shield of Faith, for the darts you meet.
Wear the Helmet of Salvation . . .
Now God's armor is complete.
Wield the Sword of the Spirit,
The Holy Word of God.
Forward March! Christian Soldiers,
As across the world we trod.
We are soldiers of the cross,
A mighty Savior, we do serve.
We are Heavenly Crusaders,
Spreading God's Holy Word.
We are Heavenly Crusaders,
Spreading God's Holy Word.

A Floppy Old Hat

One night as I was sitting quietly . . . .
My thoughts came to rest on you.
I looked at the yarn, that I held in my lap.
Suddenly . . . . I decided to make you hat.
So, I crocheted a circle . . . . added a row or two . . .
Then, I added more rows and I watched . . . as it grew.
Soon, I picked it up and turned it . . . both this way and that.
Oh my . . . it only looked like, a floppy old hat!
I went back to work . . . added a few more rows . . .
Well . . . I added . . . quite a few.
And as I watched . . . it grew and grew.
Then, I picked it up and turned it around and around,
And as I looked at it . . . from both this way and that . . .
It still just looked like a floppy old hat!
Soon, I knew . . . I had enough.
So what to do next? Well, that was tough!
I grabbed some flowers and ribbons.
I sewed them on to the crown of the hat.
Then, I turned it . . . both this way and that . . .
But it still just looked like . . . a floppy old hat!
Something was missing . . . that I couldn't think of.
Suddenly, I knew! I grabbed a handful of love!
I stuffed the little hat full and attached a back.
Now, I turned it . . . both this way and that.
Finally! It looked like . . . . A pretty hat!
One thing more . . . I added . . . a hanger , , , that's all.
Now it will sit on a table . . . or hang on the wall.
As you look at it . . . from both this way and that . . .
Remember . . . it was once . . . just a floppy old hat.
Then remember . . . what it is full of . . .
And you'll know . . . that your pretty little hat . . .
Was made . . . just for you . . . with lots of love.

I Learned It From You

When I was just a baby, I learned a trick or two.
I'd cry, you'd pick me up, then I'd laugh and coo.
Cute trick?? I learned it from you.
Soon, I could sit up, then you taught me how to crawl, too.
You'd make a bridge with your legs and I'd go through.
You thought, I was so bright! . . . but, I learned it from you.
Next, I learned to stand and take a step or two.
You held out your arms and I'd toddle over to you.
Wow! I could walk! And I learned it from you.
I soon learned to talk and say words . . . when I wanted to.
Most of the words were simple, but I said some bad ones too.
Ohhh, naughty, naughty . . . but I learned it from you.
Soon it was time for me to go to school.
I could say my ABC's, knew my colors and . . . .
I could print my name too.
You showed me how to do all this . . . I learned it from you.
Next came the pre-teen years, with phone calls, . . .
Friends . . . and a lot to do.
Sometimes at parties, we'd share a joint or two . . .
No big deal!!! . . . I learned it from you.
Then came High School, with clothes, games, dances . . .
And girlfriends and boyfriends too.
Parties were more wild, with drinking and sex
And a lot more drugs to do.

But a party is a party! I learned it from you!
I graduated, got a job and moved into my own apartment too.
You began to go to church, you wanted me to go with you.
I was too busy for that . . . I learned that from you.
Last night, I went to a party, that I was invited to.
Many of them were snorting coke . . . so, I did it too.
Big Mistake! I over dosed . . . But I learned it from you.
Now here I lie, I saw you come in . . . .
I prayed with you, in my head.
Mom? Dad? I can't feel anything! I just heard the doctor . . .
He just told you that, I'm dead.
If I could talk, there's one thing that I would do . . .
I'd tell you that all the things, I learned on Earth . . .
I learned it all from you!
Love, Your Child

Did You?

When you woke up this morning . . .
Did anyone see you . . . bow your head to pray?
When you heard those swear words or dirty jokes . . .
Did you stay and listen, or did you walk away?
Were you friendly, to the new guy on the block?
Did you offer to show him around?
Or did you leave him standing alone,
Puzzled and alone . . . just staring at the ground.
Did you invite him to church . . .
Or to a Bible study, with you?
Were you friendly? Did you show God's love?
Remember . . . like the new guy . . . you were alone once too!
Reach out to others quietly, don't judge and don't be pompous.
You know that God, shows His love . . . through us.
Spread God's word, by the life you lead.
Lend a hand, when you see someone in need.
So now, dear friends . . . I'm asking you,
Did you do today, what God expected you to?
Did you make God smile and bless His heart,
By spreading His word and doing your part?
Did you plant a seed today . . . in this world, for God?
Did you plant a seed today, wherever you chanced to trod?
Did God count on you, to talk to that brother in need?
But did you shrug your shoulders . . .
And did you walk away . . . instead of planting a seed?
Hmmmmmmm?

A Prayer

Our Father in Heaven, we are in agreement, as we petition You
We pray and ask that You will cause us to desire . . .
Only the things, that are pleasing to You.
Please anoint us, with your Holy Spirit,
Each day, as we get out of bed.
May only the things that bring You praise and Honor and glory,
Be the things, that fill our head,
Teach us to live each day as if it were our last day on Earth.
And to do all we can for You Lord,
And to do it for all we're worth.
We can do nothing to repay You, for all You do for us each day.
Father use us as Your tools.
Show us how to serve You, in any way.
Yes, Please use us Lord, in any way You can.
And Father, show us how to fit into Your Master Plan.
We want to thank You God, for Jesus, Your only Son.
We thank You, Jesus, for caring for us and our daily needs,
And for all the things, You've done.
Thank You for sending Your sweet Holy Spirit,
To convict us and convince us of our sin.
Thank You Holy Spirit, for prodding us and keeping us in line,
Whatever situation, we're in.
Father, Please let the Holy Spirit fall heavy . . .
On all who are here tonight.
And thank You Jesus, that we are precious, in Your sight.
We give You all honor and glory and praise, . . . each day.
And it is . . . . in Jesus name, . . . we pray.
Amen

My All In All

How many times Lord, must I slip and fall . . .
Before I give You . . . my all in all?
My temper flies . . . a bad word slips out . . .
Please dear Father, Please turn me about.
My friends tell me their problems. I listen and pray,
For Your wisdom. That I may guide them . . . Your way.
I get so upset when folks don't come to church . . .
To worship You.
They don't act . . . like You want them to.
But then, am I the good witness . . .
That You want me to be?
Are You really, so very proud of me?
As I bow my head . . . on Your name I call.
Please hold me up, lest I slip and fall.
Let me be a good witness . . . that I may walk tall.
Dear Lord, Help me . . . to give You . . . my all in all.

Kneel And Pray

Are you lost? Have you gone astray?
Are you ready for Jesus, if He comes today?
Kneel and Pray!
Has He cleansed you of your sins?
And washed them white as snow?
Have you side stepped God, my friend . . . .
Or don't you really know?
Have you slipped into a life of sin?
Is it painted black?
If you've side stepped God, my friend . . . .
Won't you please come back?
As I looked on you today, I saw you painted gray!
Have you fallen by the wayside?
Have you lost your way?
Kneel and Pray!
Won't you count the blessings, God has given you this day?
Don't you hear Him call you?
Can't you hear Him say . . .
Come, My child, I love you!
Come . . . and . . . Kneel . . . and . . . Pray!

As I Recall Thanksgiving

I recall Thanksgiving Day, at Grandma's house,
When I was a child of nine or ten.
We had ham and turkey or duck and all the trimmings,
Things were different, way back then.
The ladies, donned their aprons and gathered in the kitchen . . .
To prepare this festive meal.
The men were in the living room . . . discussing . . .
Football, politics, farming and their latest "deal".
Older children, helped set the table,
Adding their home made decorations,
To make it look "just right."
Then Grandma would announce: "Dinner's Ready."
"Come to the table now, before it gets cold."
So, we all hurried to the table, both young and old.
By that time, were all hungry enough to eat a bear.
So it didn't take too long, to find a chair.
As we all sat down, each head was bowed in prayer.
Thanking God . . . for His bountiful blessings, and the food,
Our good health and for everyone who was there.
We asked Him to bless the poor and the needy,
And to bless the sick and make them whole,
To touch the hearts of the lost and to save each soul.
With hands and hearts joined together, we all prayed the same.
And we asked all of these things . . . in Jesus name.
I pray each of you will build fond memories,
As you go along life's way.
And may each of you have . . . .
A very Happy and Blessed, Thanksgiving Day!

Revive

Revive me again, Oh Father Devine.
Take my life, make it more like Thine.
If I should backslide and go astray,
Just reach down, take my hand,
And have Thine own way.
Revive me, dear God.
I know You're right there.
I've had so many problems lately,
I didn't take time for prayer.
Will You forgive me, dear God,
For everything, I've done?
I know You love me God,
For me, You gave Your only Son.
I know, I haven't done Your will.
I've been a sinner, in every way.
Please forgive my forgetting You,
Amid my trouble and strife,
And God, I promise, to try to walk . . .
And let You guide me . . . each day . . .
For the rest of my life.

Why Wonder?

When I sit and wonder and I have a little doubt,
If I have some trouble, figuring out . . .
Just what my life, is all about,
I have to ask . . . .
Do I do all I can, for You, my Lord . . .
To show Your love and spread Your word?
Do I share what I have, with my fellow man?
Father, am I truly doing all I can?
Do I encourage others, when they are sad? . . .
And share with them, the experiences, I've had? . . .
The things that draw me closer to You . . .
And the faith You give me, to see me through?
The forgiveness, that You've shown me . . .
The love, You give . . . unconditionally.
Lord, I no longer wonder . . . .
And I no longer doubt.
I'm putting my life in Your hands Lord,
Because . . . You . . . have it all planned out.
Thank You, Jesus.

Do Your Father's Work

Make Your Father proud of you.
Do things, the way He'd want you to.
Do everything, for glory to Your Fathers' name.
You'll have God's love,
You won't need, mans' fame.
The pride you feel, will be a humble one.
You'll hear Him say, "Job well done!"
When you work for your Father, don't dwell on pride.
Just shine for God, don't let His light, within you, hide.
Stand out and say, "I'll work for my Father, up above."
Everything I do, I'll do with love.
And when someday, a soul, I've won.
I'll hear Him say, "That's a job well done."
I'll work for my Father and you can too.
With understanding love, He'll show you what to do.
So, in all you do, Pray to God above.
And He'll bless you greatly,
With His endless love.

My Prayer

Dear God,
Here's my life, Have Thine own way!
Please use me Lord, somehow each day.

Thank You God, for the beauty . . .
I find, in all that I see.
Thank You also Father,
For my constant walk, with Thee.

Lord, when I stagger and fall,
Please continue to pick me up.
Let me be ever thankful, God,
For the blessings that over runneth my cup.

Please accept my offerings of love, every day,
And let me always . . . remember to pray.
And dear God, Please, forever, Have Thine own way!
Amen

Phone Call To A Loved One

I called a loved one on the phone tonight.
I just called to see, if everything was alright.
The voice on the other end . . . told me . . .
"Well . . . things aren't really going so good . . .
My wife and kids and I, we aren't living, like we should."
"My teenage son . . . he hates me . . . and . . . school.
He's started to smoke "pot" and he's taken to drink.
Things have gotten bad here . . . .
In fact, worse than I care to think."
"Some years ago, I discovered,
My wife was buying and smoking dope."
"But I thought . . . Oh, it's just something "New",
And she'll soon tire of it . . . . I hope!"
But then, her "Need for weed" . . . just grew and grew.
I became confused and disheartened . . . I didn't know what to do.
Satan, confused me and enticed me . . . so I began to drink.
I thought if I got numb enough . . . I wouldn't have time to think.
Whenever we argue . . . and that's a lot . . . . anymore!
We both scream "Divorce" just to even up the score.
Dear God in Heaven,
I just can't face her and the kids leaving me.
All I've worked for these past years . . . has been for my family.

There was a time that I went to church,
The kids went with me too! . . .
But my wife . . . she wouldn't go . . .
She always had other things to do.
Finally, the kids didn't want to go either.
They'd rather stay home and play.
Soon, we all stayed home and church . . . just went by the way.
Oh, I watch the Gospel preached on Sunday morning . . . on T.V.
But I sit and watch it alone . . . no one watches with me.
So now Lord, My spirit is so low, I don't know what to do.
That's the reason . . . Dear Jesus . . . that I'm coming back to You.
Dear God in Heaven, Please hear my prayer.
Every time I pray , . . . I know, You're right there.
Lord, please forgive me, for my sins against You.
Lord, Please show me . . . what You want me to do.
Help me to stop drinking and show me how to be . . .
The kind of Christian husband and Dad . . .
That You planned for me.
You died on the cross, for my sins to atone.
God, You know what's in my heart, each and every day.
Father, I love You and I love my family.
Please heal our family and keep us together . . . In Jesus name I pray.
Amen

Hello God

Hello God . . . It's me again,
And I don't know where to start.
Well, first of all . . . Please forgive me . . .
For the grudges, I've held in my heart.
You know that phone call . . .
When "NO" was the response, I got?
Lord, you know that hurt me . . . .
I got angry . . . and my temper really got hot.
Then there was that sharp retort . . .
When unkind things were said . . .
And You know that it was a false report . . .
When I blamed it on a pain in my head.
God, You know lately, I've been all out of sorts.
It feels like my world's falling apart.
Jesus . . . Please . . . will You once again . . .
Be first place in my heart?
You know about all these things, that I've held inside . . .
That I didn't want to admit to . . . and that is foolish pride.
It all made me feel ugly and terribly mean.
Now . . . I admit my guilt . . . and I want to be clean.
Dear Father, Please forgive me,
I know that You love me God,
And that You hear my every prayer.
To be just and loving and kind and forgiving . . .
That's what I want to be.
Sweet Jesus, fill me with Your love and joy . . .
And make me more like Thee!
Put sweetness and kindness and love, in my heart.
Fill me with Your sweet Holy Spirit . . .
Once again, "Set me apart."
Lord, Please lead and guide me . . .
In all I do and say . . .
And it is in Jesus name, I pray.
Amen

I Am . . . I Am God

I Am . . . The Almighty, The Merciful, The Father.
I Am . . . . Jehovah, Yehwah and the Creator.
I Am . . . The Giver of Life and all good things.
I . . . . Even gave the angels, their wings.
I Am . . . to be honored and obeyed!
I Am . . . The Great I Am!
I Am . . . . God!
And My last name . . . is Not dam.

How I See God

I see You God . . . You're all around me.
You're in everything . . . the eyes can see.
I see Your Glory shining, as the sun rises, over the hill.
I feel Your loving Peace, as the sun sets at night, . . .
And all is still.
Your gentleness is felt, in the summer rain.
I have known Your tenderness . . .
As You lovingly, relieve my pain.
I view Your magnificent artistry . . .
And how You've painted Your canvas of Earth.
The unique colors, blending and contrasting . . . .
Ever increasing, the masterpiece's worth.
I see Your cleansing breath, as it blows across the land . . .
To either cover it up . . . or lay it bare.
Majestic waters . . . they flood . . . at Your command . . .
Often erasing, the corruption, that's lying there.
Thank You, my God and My Father . . .
For the beauty and wonder, You've put on Earth for man.
I marvel at the intricacies, of Your plan,
Thank You, for Your Son Jesus . . .
Who lived and died for man.
Lord, Please, help me to always . . .
Share Your word and show Your love . . .
In any way I can.

Save My Loved One

I'm not a professional poet and I don't profess to be.
The words, I give to you my friends,
Are the words, God gives to me.
I don't mean to hurt you, or step on anyone's toe.
But if the words apply to you, only you and God will know.
Some time ago, a prayer came into my heart,
For some folks that I hold dear.
Last night, God told me, to repeat that prayer,
Tonight, for all of you to hear.
Dear God, Please save my loved one.
I can feel him slipping away. He's drifting,
Lord, he's drifting, farther and farther away.
I need him here beside me, the way it used to be.
We worshipped You together, My loved one and me.
I stand here to sing Your praises,
With my friends, both tried and true.
But Lord, I want my loved one here,
To sing those praises too!
Please let him come and stand beside me,
For just a little while.
Then let the Holy Spirit guide him,
As he steps into the aisle.
Please God, bring my loved one, to the Christian way of life.
So we can worship You, together, God!
I love him! . . . .
I'm his loving wife!

How Much Do I Love Thee?

Dear Jesus, How much do I love Thee?
How much am I willing to give?
You gave up Your Heavenly home . . .
And Your very life . . . that I might live.
Can I give more freely of my time and talent,
That others may learn of You?
Shall I sell all and follow Your footsteps?
Lord, what would You have me to do?
Where's the cross, I am to carry?
What burden, must I bear?
What gift have I to offer?
How can I show that I care?
My sweet loving Jesus, I love You.
Please tell me . . . what shall I do?
I want to follow the footsteps You trod . . .
The ones that will lead me, to Heaven and God.
You gave me ears to hear Your word.
You gave me eyes to see.
You put a song, within my heart . . .
And I can pray, on bended knee.
When I was of the world . . . full of sin and lost . . .
Dear Lord, You never once . . . asked about the cost.
When I asked Your forgiveness . . . You pardoned me.
You gave Eternal Life . . . so sweet and free.
With love . . . You gave these things to me . . .
Now, I wonder . . . Dear Jesus . . .
How much . . . Do I love Thee?

The Little Vessel

There once was a little vessel,
It was ornate and frilly and swirled.
You could tell by the way it was painted,
It really belonged to this world.
It was passed from hand to hand,
It traveled to many parts of this land.
It got chipped and marred and tainted.
And too often, it was repainted.
The little vessel had been used for many things.
It carried whiskey and wine and all kinds of sin,
Which marred it on the outside,
And stained it deep within.
Then one day, it stood alone,
And cried out with great despair.
Won't somebody help me? Doesn't anybody care?
Then a man, who saw the vessel,
Thought it had some worth.
He took the vessel to church with him,
And prayed, each Sunday morn,
That God would remove, the worldly marks,
That the vessel, for so long, had worn.
The stains began to fade away and it began to shine.
And then one day, as it was touched,
By the word of God, Devine . . . .
The Holy Spirit, filled it up and it went down the aisle.
The vessel was so excited, it poured out tears,
And then . . . a smile.
The vessel is all new again, it knows it has some worth,
As it goes spilling God's word, as long as it's on Earth.
Yes, God cleansed the little vessel,
And made it just like new.
And if you only ask Him,
He'll do the same for you!

So Many Words To Choose From

So many words to choose from,
I don't know where to start.
I know, I'll ask my Father,
On my own, I'm not too smart.
So many words to choose from,
Just how can I impart,
The beautiful message, God gave me,
That I hold, here in my heart?
So many words to choose from,
So many words to say.
I know the words You mean, Dear Lord,
But please, just teach me Thy way.
So Many words to choose from,
They've been there all this day.
I don't know how to use them all.
I know . . . I'll kneel and pray.
Dear Heavenly Father, up above,
Please help me tell them of Your love.
What You did for others, You did for me.
You sent Your Son, to set us free,
To free us from our burdens and woe,
For all our sin, His blood, did flow.
Yes, You so loved the world, You gave your only Son.
When He died, He cleansed our sins,
When He said, "It's Done!"
Dear Father, forgive me the sins of this day.
Humbly I beg You, just touch my heart . . .
And teach me to pray.
Amen

Waiting For The Rapture

I am waiting for the Rapture,
Meanwhile, I want to capture . . . many a soul.
I want to tell everyone, about Jesus . . .
How He cleansed and made me whole.
Yes, I'm waiting for the Rapture.
I want to see His Holy face.
I've just got to tell people about Jesus . . .
And about His saving grace.
When I was of the world and living in sin . . .
I envied the Christian . . . the peace, they had within.
I began to go to church, I listened and I learned.
I learned, why Jesus died for me . . .
And about the love, I'd spurned.
I opened my heart and asked Jesus to come in.
Then I cried for joy, as He washed away all my sin.
Are you ready for the Rapture?
Do you know where you will go?
Have you accepted Jesus?
Has He cleansed and made you whole?
Oh Sinner, it's for you I plead.
Open your heart to Jesus . . .
He's all you ever need.
Yes, I'm waiting for the Rapture.
I know where I will go,
For I've accepted Jesus . . .
He is the Savior of my soul.
Are you ready for the Rapture?
Do you really know where you will go?
Won't you accept my Jesus?
Oh sinner, Don't say no!
I'm begging and I'm pleading . . .
Accept Jesus and let Him
. . . . Save your soul!

Too Late

I as I looked at the young man, my sorrow was deep.
My heart was so sad . . . it began to weep.
I tried to win him to Jesus.
I tried to show him . . . God's way.
He said, he just wasn't ready . . . but maybe another day.
He had sweet children and a lovely wife . . . .
Yet things of the world . . . .
Were in control of his life.
They asked him to go to church with them.
They tried with all their might.
They would ask him on Sunday morning . . . .
And again, . . . on Sunday night.
He would go, on rare occasions . . .
But he'd rather watch T.V. or stay in bed.
He'd be nursing a hangover,
And the pounding in his head.
I asked him to accept Jesus . . . before it was too late.
His sweet little family, was already saved . . .
So he knew, ... Their Eternal fate.
I tried and tried, with all my might.
He said, "I'm just not ready . . . not tonight."
I went home and prayed and then I cried,
Although, I knew, I really had tried.
The next morning, he went to work, just like any other day.
Someone wasn't watching, they didn't know he was in the way.
Someone hit the wrong pedal . . . it was a grave mistake.

They had hit the gas, when they should have hit the brake.
The young man, lay deathly quiet,
As he lay in that hospital bed.
His family gathered around him, praying . . .
But by morning . . . the young man was dead.
My heart is breaking, for I know . . . now, it is too late!
I'll never again hear him say . . .
"No, I'm not ready . . . not tonight . . . I'll wait."
So friends, you know what you have to do . . . .
Accept Jesus . . . NOW . . . before it's too late . . . . for you!!

Voice Of A Sinner

Dear God, I'm lost, . . . won't You show me the way?
I'm so lost, I can't remember how to pray.
Now what would God want, with a sinner like me?
I've been about as sinful, as I can be!
I'd have come to church on Sunday . . .
But I went out, ... on Saturday night.
Well, You know God . . . I drank too much,
And then there was that fight.
You know God, it really wasn't much fun for me.
It's just not like it used to be.
Say, look here now, what am I doing on my knee?
What's that You say? There's still a chance for me?
Even me? Now? Today? . . . .
If I ask for forgiveness and confess before men?
Dear God, I'm sorry, forgive me this day,
And I'll confess before men . . . Just show me the way!
Oh God, by the way, Thank You!
For letting me . . . a sinner,
Remember . . . . How to pray.
Amen

And I Was Worried

Here we sit, just God and me.
He's teaching me to write poetry.
I've been down in the mouth, as of late.
So many bills, with a "Past Due" date.
I worried and I'd sit and stare.
Now, I'm handing them over to Him . . .
To handle, with His wise care.
I don't know what to do . . .
Or where the money's coming from.
I only know, He's got "em now!
My worrying is done!
I'm asking God, Please help me climb these great big hills.
Since I've asked Him, I know I'll find . . .
Some way to pay these bills.
Oh God, Please help me pay for this or that.
Boy, I'll bet to Him, by now . . .
It really seems "Old Hat."
But what I keep forgetting . . .
Is to ask and to believe . . . His promise to us, that says . . .
"Ask . . . and Ye shall receive."

It's Easter

We celebrate Easter, with new clothes . . . and family
And Easter baskets . . . and . . . a delicious dinner.
Then the children have an Easter egg hunt.
Whoever finds the most eggs . . . is the winner.
But what is Easter anyway?
Is it only . . . "Just another Holiday?"
On a hill far away . . . there's and old rugged cross.
It's an emblem of suffering and pain.
How I love that old cross, where my Jesus,
Laid down His life . . . . For my gain.
Oh yes, that old rugged cross, made the difference.
But wait! That old rugged cross,
Was made from the wood of a tree.
It was Jesus, who died upon that cross.
He made the difference . . . for you and for me.
Yes, God sent His Son, they called Him Jesus.
He came to set us free!
He came to this Earth, as a wee tiny baby.
As an adult, He spent three years, going from city to city . . .
Pursuing His ministry.

As He walked among us, He healed the sick, the lame, the blind,
And he cast out demons too!
He never sinned in all His life, every word He spoke, was true.
His last days on Earth, were a shameful disgrace.
He was tried before Pilate, beaten, mocked and spat upon.
They even pulled the beard, from His face.
He laid there, without a sound,
As they nailed Him to that tree.
He willingly, laid down His life that day.
He did it, for you and me.
He said "I'll die upon that cross . . . but I will rise again!"
"I'll go to Heaven . . . I'll sit at My Father's right hand."
Then, He sent the Holy Spirit . . . so He could do His part . . .
To prick our conscience and prod our heart.
So my friends, Let's truly celebrate this Easter Day.
Let's claim Jesus as our Savior!
He is the Life, the Truth and The Way.
Right now . . . today . . . won't you ask for forgiveness of your sin?
Open your heart's door and ask Jesus to come in.
He will lighten your burden and ease your strife.
You will also have . . . Eternal Life.
Won't you come now . . . and go Jesus' way?
It would make this . . . your most "Special" Easter Day!!

Would It Be Enough?

Dear Heavenly Father,
I've been thinking, of all You do for me.
If I were to give up something, to further Your Kingdom,
What would it be?
I could give up, all of my material things,
That wouldn't be so tough!
But . . . all of my material things? Would it be enough?
What would I give, to further God's Kingdom?
Well, now let me see . . .
What could I give up?
What means the most to me?
I could give up my eyes, . . . and never more see . . .
A smile, or the beauty all around me.
Yes, I could give up my eyes . . . . That would be tough! But still . . . .
Would it be enough?
I could give up my ears . . . and never more hear you sing,
Nor hear a bird, or a baby's laughter . . .
Just never more hear anything!
Not to hear? That too would be tough!
But still . . . . Would it be enough?
Perhaps, my husband and my family . . .
To give up their loving embrace?
Oh, Dear God above . . . to even give up their love?
Now That would really be tough!
But still . . . . Would it be enough?
Then . . . a thought occurred to me.
God didn't ask me to give up anything, you see.
He sent His Only Son, to die for me!
Now that was Super tough!!!
But still . . . you just sit there . . . lost and in sin.
I guess . . . it still . . . was not enough!

Who Cares . . . . Do You?

I'm despondent today . . . I'm really blue.
I know . . . who cares? Do You?
I just got laid off, the whole factory shut down.
I checked and there isn't a job to be found.
I really don't know what we're gonna do . . . .
But then . . . who cares . . . Do you?
Think I'll head for the bar, and tip a few.
I'll talk to the guys and see what's new.
We're all goin" there for one last fling . . . .
Why with this little check . . . I can't pay anything.
My wife'll be upset . . . cause the old rent is due . . .
Ahhhh! Who cares? Do You?
Hmmm . . . There's that little church again . . .
Wonder what's the big ado.
Why the lights are on, and the bell's ringing too!
Think I'll stop for just a minute and slip on in.
Huh!! . . . there he goes already . . . a harpin" on my sin.
If he don't hush . . . I'll leave . . . that's what I'll do.
So anyway . . . Who Cares? Do you?
Why, say now . . . he just pointed at me and said . . .
"Jesus loves you!"
Hey . . . . Am I the one he's talking" to?

Hmmm . . . Jesus died on the cross, to save sinners like me?
Well . . . I'm not livin" . . . like I ought to be.
The preacher said, "If you raise your hand . . .
We'll pray for you."
Okay, I'll raise my hand, if someone sees me . . .
Oh well!! . . . Who cares? Do You?
Ya" know . . . I really would like to have Jesus in my heart,
He'd clean up my life and give me a new start.
Think I'll go down and kneel in prayer . . .
But then . . . all those fancy dressed people . . . are gonna, stare.
Man, my heart feels like I been runnin, a race . . .
And there's tears . . . runnin, down my face.
Now I know what I gotta do . . .
Excuse me please . . . I just gotta get through.
With a tear stained face and a broken heart . . . he knelt there.
He asked Jesus to forgive him . . . in a sinner man's prayer.
Now he has something to say to you.
Praise the Lord!!! I'm Saved!!! I'm born anew!
Now . . . I know who cares . . . . Do You?

A Plea For God's People

I've come before you, to make a plea.
You people out there, mean a lot to me.
Are you right with the Savior,
Or have you fallen behind?
Do you know He loves you?
He's still the same God, forgiving and kind.
He's patiently waitng, beside you today.
Reach out! Take His hand . . .
Let Him have His own way.
Maybe you've sinned and headed down the wrong road.
He's right there beside you . . .
To forgive you and lighten your load.
We all need Jesus in our lives, my friend.
Tomorrow may be too late, today could be the end.
A short time ago, at a Revival,
I was brought down to my knees.
I asked God to forgive me, with a great big Please!
I remember vividly that beautiful day . . .
As I reached out and took His hand,
And said, "Have Thine Own Way!"
Now, you search your heart and earnestly pray!
Then, reach out . . . take His hand . . .
Let Him have His own way.

Until He Comes

Until He comes . . . what shall I do?
There's many tasks to be done, so I'll mention just a few.
We can boldly witness to others, about God's saving grace.
We each have a talent . . . to do our Father's will.
It may be the art of listening . . . that too, is quite a skill.
Perhaps we can teach a Sunday School class,
Speak gently, to each lad and lass.
You must study hard and do your part.
Show them how to take Jesus, into their heart.
We can live our lives, in a Christlike way . . .
To win many souls . . .
To Jesus . . . each day.
Until He comes . . . we can kneel and pray
Have a Bible Study, Invite your friends.
See how the list . . . just never ends?
You can visit the sick . . . in hospital or at home.
You can give to the poor . . . but don't let it be known.
Give time to the widow . . . who's lonely and blue.
How about the orphans? . . . They need love too!
Stand by your preacher . . . give help, when you can.
After all, he is God's appointed and anointed man.
Reach out to someone . . . every day,
And until He comes . . .
I'll continue to pray . . . .
For you!!

Day By Day

He knocks on the door of your heart, day by day.
Do you let Him in. or do you turn Him away?
Do you sadden His heart with your awful sin?
Or do you open the door, and let Him in?
He'll forgive your sins of scarlet and make them white.
He'll lift your heavy burdens and make them light.
If you let Him in, day by day,
He'll love you and lead you and show you the way.
He gave His Son, who died for your sin.
So won't you open the door and let Him in?
When you hear Him knocking, day by day,
Open the door to your heart, don't turn Him away.
Just open your heart and make Him smile.
Trust in Him, . . . "As a little child."
When He comes in, you'll be so proud,
You'll say "God is here!" right out loud.
Then you'll feel His touch, each time you pray,
As you gladly let Him in, day by day.

Share

We'll share with you, our home, our food and our love.
One thing more we'll share, our God, from up above.
God makes our house a "home", you see.
He constantly blesses, you and me.
Through Him we're blessed, with food to eat.
Our daily needs, He'll gladly meet.
Come and join us, pull up a chair,
With you, His blessings, we'll gladly share.
If you've a struggle, that's hard to bear,
We'll sincerely listen and we'll share.
We have God within us, we really do care.
Then together, we'll take it to Him in prayer.
God shared with us, His only Son.
He sent Him for us, for everyone!
So let God in your heart, show someone you care.
And He'll show you how easy it is . . .
To share!

Look Up

As we were riding through the countryside,
I became engrossed, in the beauty, I beheld in the skies.
It appeared as though the clouds had sprung some leaks,
The leaks, became small chasms, with soft silvery streaks,
That seemed to pierce through the clouds,
And stream downward, in a rush,
As if put there with the final downward stroke . . .
Of an artists' brush.
If one used ones' imagination, one would possibly think . . . .
That one was perhaps viewing . . .
An ever so slight . . . glimpse on the brink,
Of seeing a touch of Gods' "Shekinah Glory" . . .
shining down on this globe . . . .
Possibly emanating, from the very hem of God's robe.
How much more intense, that beauty and glory will be . . .
When we see God, face to face.
Is it any wonder, that we'll fall on our knees in praise,
When He comes to get us, from this place.

A Brand New Day

As I begin this brand new day . . .
Father help me to do things . . . Your way.
In everything, I may say or do . . . .
Let it be a loving reflection . . . of You.
As I walk with You, from morning to night . . .
Help me walk only straight and right.
With each choice I must make,
Please help me be true,
So all of my actions will be pleasing to You.
Teach me to be considerate of each sister or brother,
To show loving kindness, as a friend and a Mother.
Please grant me wisdom, as I make each choice.
Open my heart to hear that "Still small voice."
Thank You Father, for my life this day.
May I fill it with You . . . .
In Jesus name, I pray!

Let Me Be More Like You

I want to follow the footsteps of Jesus
To help my faith grow strong
As long as I lean on Jesus,
He will right everything, that's wrong.
Sweet Jesus, please lead me . . .
Through the rest of my life.
Please grant me Your strength
To face each trouble and strife.
Dear Lord, hold tight to my hand . . .
And lead me from up above.
Jesus, You loved me so much,
You gave Your life for me.
Dear God, please lead and guide me . . .
That my life will reflect . . . only Thee.
Father, please forgive me of any sin . . .
That I have committed this day.
Help me to use every minute and each hour . . .
To walk, only . . . in Your way.
Lord, You died a cruel death . . .
Just so I might live.
Theres' nothing more anyone could do . . .
Nothing more anyone could give.
Teach me Lord, more loving and honest . . .
and kind to be . . . .
So when others look upon this face . . .
They will only see Jesus, in me.
And so Dear Jesus, in all that I do . . . .
Let me be increasingly . . . .
More like You . . . . Amen

Can This Be Love

A hug, a kiss, the holding of hands,
How God must smile, from up above,
When He hears them say, "Can this be love?"
He turns to look at other places,
A busy street, with different faces,
Hurried people, they push, they shove.
There's a scowling face an angry word.
Well now, Can this be love?
Now He views a movie, with great despair.
Why, it's nothing but "sex" and not one empty chair.
Satan's in his glory, says God from above,
And where are my people? Can this be love?
Next He sees a man, who grieves for his wife.
Two thugs took her money and then her life.
What is todays' world made of?
Is it acts like these? Can This be love?
He turns again, a view to see,
In a distant land, far away, from you and me.
The land is parched, from the lack of rain.
A Mother, listens to the cries of her child,
Whose tiny body, is wracked with pain
God frowns, as He looks down from above,
Then a tear falls, Can this be love?
God looks at the world, sees the mess it's in,
After He gave us His Son, to free us from sin.
He let Him come to Earth, to set us free,
To cleanse us from sin, yes, you and me.
He let Him come down from His home, up above.
He was, The Supreme Sacrifice!
Now friend, That's love . . . .
Ultimate . . . Love!

I Am A Little Church

I am just a little church, and I want so much to grow
There's been some dissension here,
And I don't know where to go.
One time, some action got started . . .
But it fell through.
Then we had Revival. It was great . . . for a while,
Then, that failed too!
Now, my people are unhappy and I don't know what to do.
Won't everyone please pray for me?
That means you . . . and you . . . . and you! Won't somebody help me?
Please give it one more try. Although, I'm just a little church . . .
I'm still too young to die!

A Prayer From The Ill

Dear Heavenly Father, please light a light for me,
That I might see . . . beyond my pain and misery.
My prayer to You Father, as I lie here so still,
Is that You will light my way, to do Thy will.
As You look at me, Your unworthy child,
And see to my every need,
My future, every word and every deed.
With loving kindness, lift my spirit up.
Let me count the blessings, that over runneth, my cup.
Oh God, please grant me, the grace to bear . . .
The pain and the doubt, as I lie here.
I am Your child and I know that You care.
Father, I know that You won't forsake me.
I feel Your presence with me, every hour.
Thank You Lord, for the blessings,
Of Your loving, healing power.
Dear God, right now, I've nothing more to say,
Except, it is, In Jesus name I pray.
Amen

The Story Of The Samaritan Woman At The Well

When Jesus left Judea, He went to Galilee.
He went out for a special reason,
To continue His ministry.
Just out of Samaria, not too far,
He came to a city, that was named, Sychar.
This was near the plot of ground,
That Jacob gave to Joseph, his son.
Jacob gave land to all his sons, each and every one.
Now on this land, Jacob dug a well,
Then around it, built a wall.
Anyone could get water there, the well was used, by all.
The disciples left Jesus, at the well
And went to buy some food in town.
Jesus, was tired from traveling,
So He sat His weary body down.
A woman from Samaria, came to get water.
Jesus asked her for a drink . . .

She looked at Jesus, saw He was a Jew,
This made her stop and think.
She said, "I'm a woman of Samaria,
Why ask me for a drink? You're a Jew!
Jews have no dealings with Samaritans . . . why do You?"
Jesus answered, "If you knew of God's gift and who I am,
that asks you for a drink . . . you would have asked Him
and He would have given you . . . . "Living Water."
"Now, what do you think?"
She said to Jesus, "Sir, you have nothing with which
to draw water and the well is deep.
From whence will You get this water . . . .
the "Living Water," that You keep?"
She asked, "Are You greater than our father Jacob?
He gave us this well.
He and his sons drank from this well, so did his cattle."
Jesus, had her thinking now, that was half the battle.
I'll paraphrase now, for just a time,
To get the next few verses, into this rhyme.
"Woman, hear me now, whoever drinks of the water from this
well, will thirst again, regardless whether it's a man or woman,
or husband or wife. But whoever shall drink of the water that
I shall give him, shall never thirst. But the water that I give him
Shall be in him, a well of water, springing up into everlasting life."
The woman said to Jesus, "Sir, give me this water, so I won't
Thirst and I'll have no need of water pots to carry."
But Jesus said, "Go call your husband, then come here,
Go and do not tarry!"
She said, "But a husband . . . I have none."
Jesus said, "This is true, you've had five, not only one."
Then He told her all the things in life, she'd done.
She believed He was a prophet, she was listening closely now.
He told her about worshipping and then, He told her how.

She was so anxious to get back to the city,
She left her water pots behind.
She told them what Jesus had said.
She told everyone she could find.
Meanwhile, the disciples came back and asked Jesus to eat,
Their Master, they did love.
He told them, He had food to eat, that they knew nothing of.
They asked one another, if Jesus ate any of the food,
The food they had brought.
Each in turn, as they were asked, said that He had nought.
Jesus said, "My food is the will of My Father,
To finish the work, He sent me to do.
You say, there's four more months until harvest, now I say to you.
Lift your eyes, look at the fields, they're white and ready to harvest.
There's so much to do!
He that reaps and he that sows, rejoice together, for their strife.
Now another saying that is true, one reaps and one sows . . .
Now, I'm sending you!
You are to reap that which you bestowed no labor on.
Others labored, but you must work, until it's done!"
Many Samaritans, came from the city,
Because the woman told them what Jesus said to her.
So, when they asked Jesus to stay a couple of days . . . .
Jesus said, "I'll stay two days, for sure."
He stayed for two days, many more believed,
the precious words, He spake.
They told the woman, "We believe, not because of what you said,
It's Jesus' word, we'll take!"
After two days, He left there and went to Galilee,
To continue the work of His Father . . . .
And to continue His ministry.

The Good Samaritan

A certain man came down from Jerusalem, going down to Jericho.
Some thieves came by and robbed him, they took all he had.
Then they beat him and they left him, alone and hurt and sad.
By chance, there came along, a certain Priest that day.
He didn't help that poor sick man. He looked the other way.
Then along came a Levite and looked on that poor man's face.
He didn't help. He turned his back and quickly, left that place.
Then came a Samaritan, a kind and gentle man.
He looked at the man and said, "I'll help as best I can."
He had compassion for the poor hurt man . . .
And that's to say the least.
He bound his wounds and covered him . . .
And let him use his beast.
To the nearest Inn, they went to stay.
The Samaritan said, "Don't worry friend,
Until you're well . . . . I'll pay."
The next day, the Samaritan had to go,
No longer could he tarry!
He left some coins with the Innkeeper . . . two Denari,
Then he said, "Take care of my friend and if it costs more,
WhenI get back, we'll even up the score."
If you picked a neighbor, out of the three,
Think it over . . . . Who would it be?

Samaria

If we look on a map, we'll find,
Two lands . . . Judea and Galilee.
They were sort of, two of a kind.
In between, we find Samaria, a mixed up tribe,
Of whom the other two didn't give much worth.
But really, they were, the salt of the Earth.
The Israelites and Judeans, crossed over Jordan . . .
To visit each other.
They didn't want to come in contact,
with their Samaritan brother.
There was great animosity between the Samaritans
and the Israelites.
They often indulged, in useless fights.
So. Around Jerusalem, the Jews built a wall,
To keep out the "unwanteds . . . the Samaritans and all.
They said it was a fortress, to protect the town.
But it was built up . . . to put the Samaritans down.

Leviticus

What . . . oh what . . . does our God, expect from us?
Well, some of the instructions are found, in Leviticus.
He is a Holy God and wants us to be the same . . . .
To be obedient to His will and bring glory, to His name.
He gives clear standards . . . for living a Holy life.
And special instructions . . . for a husband and a wife.
It even tells us how to receive God's blessing.
And how to receive forgiveness, for our transgressing.
He sets the rules about handling food and disease . . .
Even sex . . . and health problems too!
He is a Holy God and we are to be Holy . . . too!
We are to devote all areas of our life, to Him and His will . . .
That means you . . . and . . . you . . . and . . . you.
We are to learn and accept His ways . . .
And stop making such a fuss.
We can learn a lot, about how to live our lives . . .
By reading . . . Leviticus.

How Strong Is Your Faith?
(Book of Job)

Our story begins in the land of Uz,
About a man named Job, a blameless and upright man he was.
He shunned evil and feared and loved, the Lord above.
Job had a family, a wife, seven sons and three daughters.
Job enjoyed good health and his large family's love.
He was also rich. He had donkeys, camels, oxen and sheep.
There were also many servants, who worked for their keep.
His sons had fine homes and often
Asked their sisters, to join them for a feast.
But it was their father Job, who was the greatest man . . . .
Among all the people of the East.
When the feast was over, with no more eating or drinking . . .
Job had them purified and sacrificed a burnt offering . . .
Because he was thinking . . . .
Perhaps my children have sinned and are set apart.
Or maybe they have even cursed God, in their heart.
This was Job's custom, after every feast.
He was truly, a great man of the East.
One day, the angels presented themselves to God . . .
And satan did too!
Then, God asked satan, "Where have you come from,
Like, what are you up to?"
Satan said, he had been going back and forth, through the Earth.
God told him to consider his servant Job, a man of high worth.
God said, "He loves Me. He shuns evil. He's blameless and upright."
Satan said, "Yeah , . . . Sure . . . You've given him everything!
He has no reason to be "uptight."
But if You stretch out Your hand and strike his household
and all his . . ." Things" . . .
Why, he'll curse You to Your face. His faith will have wings."
God told satan, "Very well then, everything he has is in your hand,

But satan, as far as Job himself, . . . don't lay a finger, on the man."
Then satan left God's presence, to go do his "dirty work."
Because, to destroy God's people, is a job, he'll never shirk.
Now the scene changes, as we knew it would . . .
And satan's already up to no good.
Job's children are eating and drinking,
At the home of his oldest son,
When a messenger came to tell Job,
His donkeys and oxen have been stolen . . . every single one.
They also killed your servants, with a sword,
Only I escaped . . . to bring you this word.
Just then, another messenger came to say,
"The fire of God, fell from the sky.
It burned up your sheep and servants . . .
Only one escaped to tell you . . . and that is I.
Still another messenger, came to tell Job,
His camels were stolen and they killed the servants too.
He said, "I am the only one who escaped, to come and tell you."
Yet one more messenger came, to strike another blow.
It pulled at Job's heartstrings, and filled him full of woe.
He told Job, "Your children were eating and drinking,
At the home of your oldest son,
When a mighty wind blew in and struck his house.
It collapsed . . . . killing everyone.
This message is very sad . . . it's true . . .
But I am the only one who escaped, to tell you."
Job was so sad, that his family was dead . . .
He got up and tore his robe and shaved his head.
Then he fell to the ground . . . in worship . . . and he said . . .
"Naked I came from my Mother's womb and naked, will I depart."
"The Lord gave and the Lord, has taken away,
May the name of the Lord, be praised."
Now, although Job's heart was heavy and he was sad within . . .
He didn't charge God with wrong doing. He still didn't sin!
So, how strong is your faith? Is it strong or does it waiver?
Look up my friend, and Rejoice! Put your faith in the Savior!

Moses And The Burning Bush

Moses, worked for his brother-in-law, Jethro.
He was the keeper of the stock.
One day, he went to the backside of the desert . . .
Just Moses and his flock.
That's where he came to Mt. Horeb . . . the mountain of God.
He saw a miracle . . . right there . . . on that sod.
There, he saw a burning bush. It was all aflame,
And in its midst . . . the angel of the Lord, came.
Moses was so surprised. He stopped and did a turn.
For although the bush was on fire . . . still, it did not burn.
When God saw that Moses, had seen the flame . . .
He called out to Moses. He called him by name.
God said, "Moses, Moses . . . I am here . . .
But you stay right there . . . don't come near."
God told Moses, "You're standing on Holy Ground."
Moses, hid his face . . . he didn't look around.

Moses knew this was Holy Ground . . . where upon, he trod.
Still, he couldn't lift his eyes and look on the face of God.
God said, "I am the God of Abraham, Isaac and Jacob . . . it's true."
"But now, Moses, I have something for you to do."
"I've seen the afflictions of My people in Egypt . . .
And I know their every sorrow.
I've come to deliver them, out of the Egyptians hand,
To take them to a place . . .
Flowing with milk and honey . . . a good land . . .
Therefore, I'm sending you . . . .
To go and see . . . . the Pharoh,
Tell him, that the God of your fathers said,
"Let my people go!"

After Thanksgiving ... What Then?

Families gather, bringing food and good wishes.
Tables are filled with all those holiday dishes.
Adults speak of work, world affairs and . . . well . . . everything.
The children are discussing, what Santa will bring.
As we sit at the table . . . .
We thank God, for His love, our food and each other,
For each child, Dad and Mother . . . .
And grandparents and each sister and brother.
We pray for those on the battlefield . . .
And the missionaries too.
Also the sick and afflicted, they need our prayers too.
All the food was delicious and dessert was fine.
I was too full . . . to eat all of mine.
Then . . . the meal was over.
The food was put away and dishes were done.
There was much laughter, as the children had fun.
Soon, it was over, everyone went home.
We sat in our easy chairs, relaxed, full and alone.
As we sat there, the house was quiet,
No more giggles and nary a shout.
We finally knew, what Thanksgiving, is all about.
It doesn't last for just this day.
Each day, should end . . . just this way.
Giving thanks to God, for His love and for each other,
For each child, Dad and Mother,
For grandparents and each sister and brother,
For those on the battlefield and missionaries too.
And for the sick and afflicted, that need prayer too.
Thank God, for all things, whatever you do . . . .
Because what ever happens . . . it's in God's plan, for you.
So, every day . . . . Thank God!

When May I Cry?

My oldest son came to me, with a tear in his eye.
He said, "I want to join the Army, Mom, I gotta try."
I had to be strong . . . as we said good bye.
And as we stood face to face . . .
I put my smile back in place.
But inside . . . I wanted to die . . .
As I asked myself . . . "When may I cry?"
Then my sweet daughter came to my room one day.
She cried and told me . . . she was in the "family way."
I tried to comfort her . . . I really did try.
We held each other closely . . . then face to face.
I tried to put my smile back in place . . .
But my heart was breaking! I felt, I could die . . . .
As I asked myself . . . "When may I cry?"
When my youngest son finds a job . . . He'll leave me too . . .
Saying . . . "Don't cry Mom . . . you know, I love you."
And as he leaves and we're face to face . . . .
I'll put that smile . . . back in its place.
But inside . . . another part will die . . .
As I ask myself . . . "When may I cry?"
Then there's my youngest daughter, now a young miss.
She's now dating boys . . . and things like this.
She wants to move to a far away land . . . .
Out of my sight and out of my hand.
Before she boards that plane and we're face to face . . .
I'll put that smile back in its place . . . .
And inside of me . . . another part will die . . .
As I ask myself . . . . "When may I cry?"
Now my husband loves me, this I know.
But there's a certain place, that we go . . .

To dance and listen to countrty music, good and pure.
But then . . . he often dances . . . . with "her."
It hurts to watch their close embrace . . .
But I keep that smile upon my face . . .
While inside, I feel, like I could die . . .
Instead . . . I ask . . . "When may I cry?"
Yes, each day . . . I wake up and continue to try . . .
But my world's falling apart. It's going awry.
But when you see me . . . face to face . . . .
I'll put my smile . . . back in its place . . .
While inside . . . each day . . . I die . . .
As I ask myself . . . . "When may I cry?"
My husband and I moved to another state.
Nice warm weather . . . I thought it would be great.
The pain has diminished from every bone . . .
But still . . . I miss my children . . . way back home.
Just a hug or a kiss from one of them, each day . . .
Or even a phone call . . . would brighten my way.
God knows . . . how I miss them and how hard, I try . . .
To cover my feelings . . . when I feel . . . I could die . . .
I'm so unhappy without them . . . When may I cry?
Through all of these trials, that I've called "My own." . . .
I've never had to face them alone.
Because God was there, to lead and to guide . . . .
Even when I felt like I was dying inside.
He gives me strength, to meet folks, face to face.
And He's the one who puts my smile in place.
Now inside . . . I know . . . I'm not going to die.
I'll just go talk to God . . . .
Then . . . . I may cry!

Thanksgiving

T—is for the Trials, You've brought me through
H—is for Heaven, where I'll one day, walk with You.
A—is for All the times, I've fallen and You've picked me up
N—is for No end to the times, You've filled my cup.
K—is for Keeping me safe and healthy, every day
S—is for Saving me and teaching me, to live Your way.
G—is for the Goodness and love, You've put in my heart.
I—is for the glorious Idea, that You've set me apart.
V—is the Victory, in Jesus, that I hold within.
I—is the Invitation, to tell all, to turn from their sin.
N—is Never, going back to the sinful road, I've trod.
G—is Giving Thanks, for all things, to our Living, Giving,
Great and Glorious God.

Our ancestors came to this country, many years ago.
They were defending their right to worship God . . . their way.
But . . . this, you already know.
The trip across the ocean, was hard and long.
Many folks wondered, if their choice had been wrong.
They were sick and hungry and some even died.
The weather was cold, not fit for man nor beast.
Then God sent some Indians to help them.
They brought all kinds of food for a feast.
They worked hard together, to prepare the food . . . all who were able.
When everything was ready, they gathered around the table.
The Indians, had a different name for God . . .
But they thanked Him just the same.
Then the Pilgrims prayed, thanking God for His loving care . . .
And for the food and the Indians, all in Jesus' name.
Now . . . if our country began with love and concern
Being shown . . . from brother to brother . . . .
Shouldn't we also, today, follow God's command
And show God's love to one another?
This year, as you gather around the table . . .
Bow your heads and pray.
Thank God for His love and His many blessings . . . to you . . . on this
Thanksgiving Day.
Have a Happy Thanksgiving and . . . .
God bless us, one and all.

Have You Ever Been Lonely

Have you ever been lonely?
Have you ever been blue?
You have a friend who cares.
He gave His life, for you.
If you knew what He went through,
Just to save your soul for you.
You'd never need to be lonely You'd never ever be blue.
Jesus, hung on Calvary.
He suffered for your sin.
But if you ask, He'll forgive you,
And make you clean within.
If you accept Jesus, friend
He'll be with you, right to the end.
You'll never again be lonely
You'll never more be blue.

On the Other Side

When I was young, I didn't belong
No matter how I tried.
Whether I was good or if I was bad . . .
I always ended up . . . . on the other side.
When I ran with the bad . . . I was a little too good
But among the elite . . . I was sort of a hood.
My many sins, I attempted to hide,
But I still ended up . . . . on the other side.
Finally, I was bad enough, to stay with the bad.
I really gave it . . . everything, I had.
The elite, shook their heads and thought they understood.
They smugly said, "Hmmph, Never was much good."
I must admit, that hurt my pride . . .
And there I sat . . . . On the other side.
Now when I grew older, I had to decide . . .
How to get back . . . . to the other side.
In my past, I had sinned, I must confide,
Then I knelt in prayer and cried and cried.
Praise the Lord, God forgave me and He touched me,
Now here I'll stay . . . . On the other side!

What Would Jesus Do?

What would Jesus do , . . .
If He walked with you today?
What would Jesus do,
Would you be proud, to have Him hear, . . .
The things you've dared to say?
Would you be ashamed, to have Him join you,
In everything you do?
Is Jesus proud of you?
Did you know, He sees your thoughts, . . .
And He hears you too?
Would you be proud, to have Him there with you?
If not, then stop and think . . .
What would Jesus do?

Secure

I am secure, in the arms of Jesus.
I am secure, In the arms of my Lord.
Whenever I have a problem . . .
I can go to Him in prayer.
I know He hears, all that I say,
For I know that He's always there.
He meets the needs, I have each day.
He lovingly leads and guides my way.
I am fed daily, by my Fathers' word,
And I am so proud to call Jesus, my Lord.
I love my God, my Father in Heaven,
I thank Him, for the peace He has given,
For sending His Son, who died for my sin,
For the joy it brings . . .
To hold Him deep within.
I am secure in Your love, Dear Jesus.
Please use me . . . somehow . . . each day.
Help me to show Your love to others . . .
For this I humbly pray.
Amen

Stain Removal

Start with one container, that is holding life.
Place this life holding container, at the altar of God.
In this container, you will find the life of one sinner.
The sinner, will indeed be stained with sin.
He will need:
1 heart, full of repentance, from deep within.
1 cup of the sinners' tears,
Shed for the sins committed, in all those years.
Cover this mixture with:
The blood of Jesus, that was shed for us all.
Add a pinch of faith, just a tiny ball.
Then fill it with truth and a daily look . . .
At the word of God . . . found in the Holy Book.
Add to this: An abundance of God's forgiveness and love,
Receive this . . . . From our Father above.
Stir this gently, but thoroughly, . . . this life will come clean.
When processed properly, upon Jesus, he'll lean.
Finish with baptism of the Holy Spirit, as soon as you can.
And show it love . . . from its fellow man.
To help this clean new life . . . stay that way,
Teach it to pray . . . many times a day.
Do Not let this freshly cleansed life, become dry and "old."
Keep it continually saturated, with the love of God . . .
And Never, Never . . . let it grow "Cold."

The Virus

I heard about a virus,
That has spread throughout the whole world.
It is now an epidemic,
As dead bodies, into the streets, are hurled.
Medical science has been working,
Endless hours . . . but so far, no cure is found.
They've searched every avenue,
Yes, they've searched all around.
Now, in one small town, there was one little boy . . .
He has been around many who were sick.
He never caught their illness.
Word of this, spread . . . real quick.
Soon the government sent medical teams,
To check this little boy out.
The boy's parents and friends and the boy . . .
Didn't know what it was all about.
They checked him over, from head to toe,
To find out, why he was so well.
Then they mixed his blood with that of the sick . . .
And their hopes, began to swell.
His blood could cure this illness, in the world, as a whole.
But would the parents allow this? The officials, did not know.
They asked the parents, if they could use the boys blood,
To cure the folks who were sick.
The parents were glad that their son's blood would help.
But their answer . . . was not so quick.
They asked, "How much of his blood do you need,
To get this great task done?"
The officials replied: "All of it, but you must understand,
He's the only one."
Now, I ask . . . What would you do?
Could you give up your only son, to save the world?
That's exactly, what God did for you!!!

Teach Me

Lord, I want to know so much . . . how do I start?
Help me to remember, that with Your love in my heart . . .
I can control my anger and not fall apart.
Teach me to swallow . . . any of those bitter words,
And show love and kindness instead.
When someone hurts one of my loved ones or me,
Please pull me up short, and take the meaness, out of my head.
Teach me Lord, how to let Your love shine, through me . . . .
And how to be loving and kind.
To be the kind of living witness, You want me to be.
Help me understand Your word, as I read every day . . . .
And how to apply it to my life, to walk only in Your way.
Each time I come to You, with a problem or care, . . .
Teach me Lord, to exercise my faith, with prayer.
Teach me not to worry, any more than a bird or a flower,
But to fully trust in Your love, Your kindness and Your Power.
Oh Lord, You know, I have so much to learn . . .
So I can be all You want me to be.
Lord, this is my heartfelt plea . . . .
Please, my Lord, Please . . . Just teach me!!

Take My "I"

Dear God, Please take the "I" out of me,
And open my eyes, that I might see.
Help me to be sensitive, to the needs of others,
To show Your love to Your children, my sisters and brothers.
Please put "You" in me, somehow, each day,
So I may tell others of Your love and show them Your way.
When doubts and fears and disappointments enter my life
And each day . . . seems to be filled with strife,
Lord, just remind me and reassure me . . . I have Eternal Life.
Sweet Jesus, help me to replace the "I" in my life,
And put You . . . in its place.
May I always remember, if I live with You, instead of "Me" . . .
There will be nothing, I can't face.
Father, help me to take the life I live . . .
And fill it with the love You give.
May all I say and all I do . . .
Be only things that will glorify You.
And if by chance, someone should ask, "Why?"
I'll tell them, "I asked God, to remove my "I."

A Special Valentine

It's Valentines' Day.
A time for hearts,
and expressions of love.
And where did all of this start? . . .
From the Master, up above.
He sent His Son to die,
that we might live.
How much more love,
Can anyone give?
Jesus, loved us so much . . .
He died, for our sin and shame.
He still loves us and will forgive us,
if we only, call on His name.
He has a much deeper love,
than yours or mine.
He was the greatest expression of love!
And certainly,
He was the first and the best . . . . Valentine.

To A Precious Valentine

My dear One,
I want to tell You, how much I love You.
But, I don't know where to start.
Words can not express this love . . .
And how full, You've made my heart.
Before we met and I fell in love with You . . .
I had wandered aimlessly and found only sinful things to do.
When I had doubt and fear, You, were always there.
When I found that I had hurt You, it was more than I could bear.
I cried, as I fell to my knees, in a sinners prayer.
But, You forgave me and lifted me up,
Showing how much You care.
You died a cruel death, upon the cross,
To prove Your love for me.
Now, for the rest of my days, upon this Earth,
I'll prove, my love to Thee.
Sweet Jesus, I thank You, for being mine.
For being my Lord and Savior and my precious Valentine!

A Valentine For My Loved Ones

To you, my family, you are so fine.
I thank God each day, for making you mine.
You keep growing more beautiful, in every way.
You're a constant reminder, that all good things,
come from God, every day.
Though we have a quarrel, or a spat or two . . .
We have love, for one another,
That is deep and true.
I thank God for all of you, in every way.
And I love you, more and more . . .
With each added, Valentine's Day.
Happy Valentines' Day.
May God bless you, in every way.
Love and prayers,
Mother

A Valentine Wish for Doctors and Nurses

To the doctors and nurses, who stood by my side,
And listened with patient understanding and care.
While my aches and pains and fears . . .
I so loudly did declare.
Thank you, for your love and devotion . . .
To the human race.
Ordinary people, can never take your place.
So, please accept my prayers of gratitude,
On this Happy Valentine's Day.
And may God's blessings be with you,
Forever . . . in every way.

What Is A Mother?

When God made woman, into a Mother
He put special things in her heart.
Each child she bears, is a part of her, you see,
And that is how God meant it to be.
To her, a baby's cry is a signal . . .
Of hurt or anger or sickness or hunger.
As the child grows, the Mother grows too.
She seems to know, just what to do.
God took the twinkle from the skies.
He put it into, a Mothers' eyes.
He took the ripple from a brook, that flows forever after.
He put that into a Mothers' laughter.
He took some gentle strength, from a tree that stands.
He put that gentle strength, into a Mothers' hands.
He took the sound of a songbird . . .
What a delightful choice.
Then, He put it into a Mother and that became her voice.
When she sits, her legs, become a lap . . . a holder,
Until you're older and need a Mothers' nice soft shoulder.
She has a way of understanding, the things you say and do.
These are just a few of the reasons, Mother . . .
For me to say . . . . I love you!!!

What the Clay Can Do With the Potter

God is the Potter. We are the clay.
He'll guide us and use us, in His own way.

Though sin may mar us and cause us much strife,
God will remold us and give us, new life.

I want to be a useful vessel, for God
Each and every day.

I'll be so proud to be of use to Him, in any way.
I'll gladly do my duty, as a mother and a wife.
As long as I have Jesus, to guide and mold my life.

Yes, if God will be my Potter,
I'll gladly be His clay,
To be His vessel, to do His work,
For this, I humbly pray.

Reality Of Aging

As I looked in the mirror,
With great dismay.
I found that my youth,
Had slipped away.
The ravages of time,
Have taken their toll.
I thank God . . . .
It's only my body . . . .
And not my soul.

I Could Have Been

I could have been a writer . . . of best selling books.
I could have been a great actress . . . with my good looks.
I could have been a singer . . . of beautiful songs,
Or maybe a Judge . . . who rights the wrongs.
I could have been a landscaper, planting pretty flowers,
Or an architect . . . who designs houses and great tall towers.
I could have been a pilot . . . flying a big jet plane,
Or an engineer . . . guiding a long fast rain.
I could have been a race car driver, with the fastest car in the race.
I could have run the Marathon. I could have taken first place.
I could have been a doctor, helping folks improve their health,
Or maybe a financier . . . helping to improve people's wealth.
I could have been President of the United States, running this country.
I could have been a brave soldier, standing against each adversary.
I could have been a missionary, maybe far across the sea.,
Or one of the greatest preachers ever. Telling folks about Jesus . . .
And how he can set them free.
Yes, ... I could have been, someone really great, you see . . . .
But then everyone said, "No, This baby is unwanted."
And so . . . . They aborted me.

© Emily Boerne

My Baby

Velvety hair and silken skin,
A turned up nose and wobbly chin.

Tiny fingers and little toes,
Today, he's so little,
Tomorrow, he grows.

Pretty blue eyes, in my baby's face,
His tiny reminders, all over the place.

My love for my baby, fills my heart,
One smile from him, can tear me apart . . .

You look at him and what do you see?
A precious angel . . .
And God gave him to me.

My Little Boy

He has flirty blue eyes,
Just as blue as the skies.
He has wavy brown hair,
And there's some devilment there.
But, he is my pride and joy . . .
Yes, he's my little boy.

He likes pots and pans,
Like most little boys.
And plays with them,
Instead of his toys.

He loves old boots
And every kind of shoe.
Yet when I despair
And feel so blue, he looks at me
And says, "Mommy, I love you."

That's when I thank God above
For giving me this son to love.
He is my pride and joy,
Yes, he's my little boy!

Heart And Soul

A sinner, was I . . . for many years.
Now, I'm smiling, through my tears.
One day, Jesus touched and made me whole.
I gladly gave Him . . . my heart and soul.
I didn't know I had a cup
Until . . . my Lord . . . had filled it up.
I asked for forgiveness of my sin,
Then I cried for joy . . . as He entered in.
My heart was heavy . . . now it's light,
For I know that I'm precious in His sight.
I've been cleansed, by the blood of Calvary.
Praise God! For His Son . . . who died for me.
Where He leads me . . . I will follow.
Where He leads me . . . I will go.
Since the day that Jesus touched me . . .
And I gave Him . . . . My heart and soul.

I Live To Serve You

I live to serve You, my Lord and my God.
To spread Your word, wherever I trod.
I kneel before You, contrite and humble.
Please forgive me Lord, whenever I stumble.
Take my hand and lead me through this life.
Grant me strength, to face this trouble and strife.
Alert me to the needs of my fellow man.
Show me how to help them, whenever I can.
Father, teach me, how to please You, each day,
To witness to someone and show them the way.
To take them out of the path of satan's snare.,
To tell them of Jesus and His love and care . . .
For too many years, I played the devil's fool.
Then I found Jesus . . . and became His tool.
He dried my tears and washed my sins away.
Now daily, I go to my Father and pray.
Please use me Lord, Oh, use me I pray!
I am here to serve You, my Lord and my God . . .
To spread Your word . . . everywhere I trod.

My Beloved One

I met a man, handsome, strong and true.
He drew me close and said, "Little One, I love you."
As I looked on His beautiful, wonderful face . . .
I never knew, such love and tenderness and grace.
He said He loved me, though I'd sinned and cheated and lied.
If I'd but ask, He's forgive me!
I felt so bad for sinning, I trembled and I cried.
I cried, "Oh, will You please forgive me?"
He answered, "Yes, I will!"
Then in the distance, I heard the voices . . . .
Angry voices . . . crying . . . "Crucify Him . . . Kill . . . Kill . . . Kill!"
They took away my beloved one, took Him up a hill.
There they nailed Him to a cross . . .
And with each nail, I heard the wail . . . .
"Crucify Him . . . Kill . . . Kill . . . Kill!
He said to me with sadness, "I die for sin."
I fell to my knees and cried and cried.
It was for my sins and the sins of the world . . .
That my Beloved Savior . . .
Was crucified.

Dear God, the Trees

As I sat at ease and took in the view . . .
The things around me . . . reflected You.
I see a grove of trees, swaying gently,
In the Autumn breeze.
The tiny seedlings . . . . just starting out,
Bend so easily, until they grow old and stout.
Some are gnarled and bent,
They lean on each other.
Others are straight and tall,
Independent of one another.
The young trees, look up to their elders . . .
In wonder and in awe, they feel like such a
Little twig. And they wonder . . . Will I ever get that big?
These trees, they mean a lot to me . . .
With their feet planted firmly in the sod.
They reach upward, ever upward . . .
Reaching to Heaven and God.
This should be an example,
To Christians, all around,
To plant their feet . . . on solid ground.
Stand up for what you believe, stand straight and tall.
Be a good witness, for the young and the small.
Be prayerful, with each step you take,
As up the road of life you trod,
Keep reaching upward, ever upward . . .
Forever . . . seeking . . . God!

I Remember Momma

Once again, Mother's Day is here.
Once again, bringing memories . . . so dear.
As a baby . . . you loved me, fed me . . . cuddled me . . .
And taught me how to sit.
Then how to crawl and stand and walk.
You taught me all of it.
Then baby language began to flow . . .
That only a Mother can understand.
When mischief entered in, as I did grow,
You employed Mother's love . . . with a firm hand.
Then came school . . . you cried, it broke your heart . . .
That first day, that we had to be apart.
Mom, I remember, every meal and bedtime,
What you used to say,
"Honey, bow your head now, it's time to pray."
When I was sick or hurt and shed lots of tears . . . .
You were there to chase away my fears.
Oh, and those teen years . . . with daily changes . . .
And the rebellion and all . . .

Mom, you were there to teach me, guide me and with love,
To comfort me, when I'd fall.
When I grew up and moved out on my own . . .
I was truly amazed . . . at how wise you had grown.
Thank you, for your faith and love and prayers . . .
Even when I was wild.
Only a Mother's love and prayers for salvation . . .
Could ever have tamed this child.
Dear Father in Heaven, Please look down from above,
And bless my Mother, with Your precious love.
If she's hurt or sick, Lord, comfort her and calm her fears . . .
And if she cries? . . . Lord, please dry her tears.
Father, Please see to her needs, as she saw to mine
Shower her today with Your blessings devine.
Lord, bless my Mother . . . in every way.
May this be her best and her happiest Mother's Day.
Amen

It's From Mother

Thank You, dear Lord, for this beautiful day.
Thank You, for the love, You've sent my way.
Thank You for my husband and children and their children too.
I know all of these blessings, come from You.
Thank You for the cards and gifts and phone calls I got.
The weather was lovely, a little warm, but not too hot.
Bless my children Lord, Don, Leo, Lori, John and Denice.
Lord grant them good health, prosperity and peace.
Please send them each . . . this heart full of love, from no other . . .
Well, just tell them . . . "It's from Mother."
Let their hearts fill with love, for one another,
And may they always remember . . . sister and brother.
Fill them with love Lord, as through life they go.
Let them feel Your presence, each day . . . help them to know . . .
That You are their God and there is no other.
Then give them this heart full of love,
And just say, "It's from Mother."
Keep them all safe from satan's evils and harms.
Lord, hold them close, in Your loving arms.
They know right from wrong, this I know . . .
So feed them Your word and help them grow . . .
Then give to them, this heart full of love . . . from none other . . .
Well, . . . just tell them . . . "It's from Mother.

Mommy

Mommy dear, O know you care!
Whenever I need you, you're always there.
In Sunday School, I learn to pray.
I thank God for you, each day.
Thank you, Mommy, for washing my clothes . . .
And fixing my food and taking care of me.
I think you're the best Mommy,
That ever, ever could be.
And Mommy?
When I'm a grown up and have lots to do,
I'll still thank God, I have a Mommy like you!
P.S. Mommy? I know you love me, in every way,
So won't you go to church with me, next Sunday?
May God bless you Mommy, I love you.
Your Child

Requiem To Mom

She was so young and beautiful as a girl.
She turned many heads and set many hearts, awhirl.
She was petite and pretty, with long dark wavy hair.
She cut a fine figure . . . she was so fair.
She had lovely dark eyes, that could talk to you.
When she was happy, they glistened, like the morning dew.
Her eyes danced and laughed . . . but they could also frown.
They could invite a man's attention . . . or . . . put him down.
She married young, to have her first child.
Everyone thought she was way too wild.
She had four children, before her marriage was done.
Three went to different homes. She was left with one.
She left him alone to run down to the store.
A neighbor called the law . . . and it was shame that she bore.
They took away this last child and that was bad.
They took him to the home of his Dad.
She married again and again and again.
All in all, she married three more different men.
The last man, was finally the right one.
Her search for true love, was finally done.
They adopted a child, to add youth to their life.
It really gave meaning, to both husband and wife.
She had much illness and trouble and strife . . .
Not only in her youth, but throughout her life.
How many times had she been misunderstood,
By those in her life . . . that termed her . . . "no good.?"

Did they know her side of the story . . . or how hard she tried?
Were they there to hold her and dry her tears, when she cried?
Now here she was, eighty six years old . . .
And oh my, how time had flown.
How many stories were lived and never told?
How many trials and pain, had this life known?
As I stood by her bed, I caressed her gray head.
Her hand lay loosely, in mine.
Her last breath was coming . . . I knew . . .
It was just a matter of time.
Then I cradled that gray head in my arms,
As she lay so still, in that hospital bed,
With tear filled eyes . . . I opened her Bible.
The twenty third Psalm, is what I read.
I held her hand as she lay there so still,
Slowly, but surely, she was losing her will.
Her eyes were unseeing, but I knew, she could hear.
So, I whispered softly, "It's all right to go now, Mother dear."
Her breathing was shallow, but still no "Death Rasp."
There was no struggle, as she breathed her last.
One breath . . . then two . . . then three . . . she was gone.
But the memories of Mom, will linger on.
It was twelve 'o four, March third was the day.
She was dying, but we sang "Happy Birthday" anyway.
We celebrated her birthday and the end of her strife.
And the angels would welcome her . . . into Eternal Life.
May she rejoice with the angels and may she be blest . . . .
And God Please grant her . . . everlasting peace and rest.

A Mothers' Day Prayer

Dear Mom,
For me, you worried, year by year.
Whenever I needed you, you were always near.

You taught me what was right from wrong.
Your constant love, made my faith strong.

Now, I'm older and the years have flown,
And it's strange, Mom.
How wise, you've grown!

I pray, God will bless you,
For what I've put you through.
"Cause Mom . . . Really and truly . . .
I do love you!!!
Love and prayers,
Your Child

Fathers are Special

Earthly fathers, come in all shapes and sizes.
Some are stern, some are routine,
Some are full of surprises.
They may be skinny or fat or tall.
The size, really doesn't matter at all.
It's what's inside his heart that counts,
I'm sure you will agree.
It's all the little things he does,
That we don't take time to see.
God put him here to guide you
And teach you of His ways.
Too often we find fault with him,
And fail to give him praise.
We forget to thank him, for paying the bills,
And when we're sick for buying our pills.
He stands by you in sickness
And troubles and fears.
He shares in your joys and your worries and tears.
When the load gets heavy and the road gets rough . . .
You may see a tear in his eye
And more gray in his hair,
As he bows his head to God, in prayer.
So, tell him today, "Thanks Dad, I love you."
He'll get a smile upon his face.
Give him a hug and a kiss and an honored place.
Let him know, he's a "Special" Dad, in a "Special" way.
Then ask God's "Special blessings for him . . .
On this "Special" Father's Day.

Dear Daddy

Dear Daddy,
I love you Daddy . . . Really I do.
And I want to learn, all the things you want me to.
I like to try new things, say new words, touch the pretties . . .
And I love to play.
Sometimes, I make mistakes though . . .
So, I thought I'd tell you so.
Like when I pick things up
That's too big for my little hand . . .
It slips . . . and falls . . . You yell . . . I cry,
Cause I con't understand.
"I didn't mean it, Daddy." Are words . . .
I don't know how to say.
Or "Daddy, I'm real sorry, you had such a bad day."
You see, I'm still little and all I know . . . is how to play.
I love it when you pick me up and I can play in your lap.
I get so excited . . . it ends up, I give a slap.
I didn't mean to hurt you, when I hit you
And it went "Kersmack."
But it sure did hurt my feelings,
When you yelled and hit me back.
There are so many things, I just don't understand.

Like . . . How did so much strength, get in a Daddy's hand?
And Daddy, why did you get so upset,
When I had that thing that gives light?
You and Mommy put it up to your mouth,
Every time you take one of those things, you bite.
When you teach me not to do, the things I shouldn't do.
Please do me a favor, Daddy . . . Will you?
If you have to spank me . . . Please use the right place . . .
Please hit me on the bottom, not in my little face.
I'm always so happy to see you, when you come home from work!
I get so noisy . . . and I want to play.
Daddy? I don't know what it means
"To work hard" or "Having a bad day."
So, you see, I have so very much to learn . . .
I just don't know what to do!
Please be patient with me, Daddy
I need you! And . . . I love you!
And . . . I'm only two.
Love and hugs and kisses,
Your little child.

Happy Father's Day

Our Father, which art in Heaven,
Happy Father's Day to You.
I pray today, that I will do . . .
Only what pleases You.

I thank You, Father, in every way,
For all the blessings, You grant me each day.
Thank You, for sending Your Son, who died for me,
When in my sin, I could have died, in hell's fiery sea.

Thank You for watching over my loved ones each day.
Teach them Father, to walk only in Your way.
Thank You Father, for Your protection, for answered prayer
And for seeing to our needs each day.

Father, I want to thank You, for keeping me . . .
And teaching me, of Your way.
And Heavenly Father, I do truly pray . . .
That You will have a very, very . . . .
HAPPY FATHER'S DAY!!!

Come To The Altar

Come to the altar and pray with me.
Don't be too proud, to get down on your knee.
Open your heart . . . let Jesus come in.
He'll love you and forgive you and cleanse you from within.
Some time ago, I asked Jesus to come into my heart.
I know now . . . I didn't give Him my all . . . only a little part.
Dear Jesus, I come to the altar today,
Heavyhearted . . . ashamed . . . . and still.
To beg You for forgiveness, Lord,
And to become submissive, to Your will.
And Lord, I know, there are others here today
Who gave You their heart . . . but not all the way.
With tears in my eyes and a heart full of despair . . .
It makes me so sad . . . when they just . . . sit there.
They each have a problem of their own . . .
But they turn away . . . saying . . . "Leave me alone."

Dear friend, come to the altar with me . . . and pray.
Please don't put it off . . . for another day.
If you're asking . . . "Do I mean right now?"
That's right! Come now! Don't wait!
Jesus may come to claim His own . . . today.
Then, it will be too late!
Please close your eyes and bow your head, in silent prayer.
Now . . . will anyone . . . come to the altar?
Please come!
Jesus is waiting . . . to meet with you there.

Thank You Jesus

Thank you Jesus, for dying for me.
Thank You Jesus, for setting me free.
I worked hard and played hard.
I didn't even try to be good.
Then one day, I realized,
I wasn't living like I should.
So, I opened my heart and asked You in.
I asked for forgiveness, of all my sin.
You forgave me and washed those sins away.
And now, I thank You Jesus, each and every day.
Thank You Jesus, for the trials,
That help me to be strong.
Thank You Jesus, for helping me to know . . .
What is right from wrong.
Thank You too, for preparing a place for me.
Each day, as I grow older, that's where I want to be.
Until then, I want to thank You Jesus,
For giving me things to do.
I'll try to work hard, here on Earth,
Doing what You want me to.
I'll watch for You and wait for You,
And until that glorious day . . .
I'll bow my head and close my eyes.
Then I'll softly say . . . . "Thank You, Jesus."

Thank God

Thank God, for birds and flowers and trees.
Thank God, for eyes and ears and noses and knees.
Thank God, for the Bible, that teaches us things.
Thank God, for angels, with beautiful wings.
Thank God, for all the food we eat.
Thank God, for all the nice people we meet.
Thank God, for everything and everyone.
Thank God too, for sending us His Son.
Thank God, for the sun and the skies so blue.
Thank God, for Mommies and Daddies . . .
And . . . Especially . . . . Thank God,
For you!!!

A Lump Of Clay

Dear God, I come to You today.
Lord, I am not much . . . just a lump of clay.
Make something worthwhile of my life, I pray.
Mold me Lord, that I walk only, in Your way.

Today, shall I be . . . someone's absent mother,
Or the caring ear of a sister to a brother?
Remind me of those, I should hold up in prayer.
If I see someone in need, help me show that You care.

I want to be . . . whatever You have in Your plan,
To bring glory to You Lord, and to benefit my fellowman.
I'm grateful for the gifts that have been bestowed on me.
Mold me and make me, that I may always use these gifts . . .
But only for Thee.

So Lord, although I'm still . . . just a lump of clay . . .
Please make me and mold me and use me . . .
Somehow, each and every day.
Thank You Lord Jesus . . . . Amen

Depression

Oh happiness, where are you?
Oh comfort, why do you elude me?
Prosperity . . . why do you flee . . .
So very far from me?
What have I done . . . that's so very bad?
Where is the joy . . . I once had?
Good health . . . are you passing me by?
Disillusionment . . . you rear your ugly head . . . .
And all I can do is cry.
I try so hard to follow God.
But I keep finding trouble, wherever I trod.
It seems, I ask "Why?" with every breath.
Will I not know comfort . . . until my death?
These tears . . . they appear . . . unbidden . . . .
From the depths of my heart . . . where they were hidden.
I know God is watching me from somewhere, out there.
But I sometimes wonder . . . "Does He really care?"
Yes, Yes, I know . . . Things could be worse . . .
But for now . . . I feel . . . I'm under some kind of curse.
So God? Won't You please hear my plea,
And bring some ease, comfort, happiness and security to me?
Father, in Heaven, my strength, is no longer of worth.
How much longer must I struggle . . .
To survive . . . on this old Earth?
All day long . . . I feel . . . I could cry.
Please help me, Dear God! . . .
Cause, I'm getting too tired to try!!!

Unworthy One

Oh Lord, I'm such a lowly servant . . .
How I desire to be more like Thee.
You're so kind, understanding and loving.
How can You bear to love, one as unworthy as me?

I'm so unworthy, I get so tired by the end of the day . . .
Sometimes . . . I even get too tired to pray.
I just lie down and say "I'm done!"
Dear God, How can You love such an unworthy one?

Please hold me close, in Your watchful care.
Guide me and prod me with love, let me know that You're there.
So. When I finish Your work and my life on Earth, is done . . .
I'll hear You say . . . "Come home, now . . . . My unworthy one."

To Encourage A Brother

My brother, my brother . . . .
Be of good cheer.
Know ye not, that the Savior is near?
Through all of our terror, Our trouble and woe,
He holds your hand.
He never lets go.
Satan may cause us pain
And disrupt our life,
With an abundance of trouble
And worry and strife.
But forge onward, my brother,
Up the prayer road, trod,
Once more . . . with faith . . .
Give your life and all that's in it . . .
Back to God!

Fireside Chat

I sat by the fireside, with my Bible in my hand,
I bowed my head and I prayed to God . . .
Please help me understand.
To be like Jesus . . . to obey Your will . . .
And to live as You want me to do.
Please fill me with Your Holy Spirit,
That I may forgive others, as You forgive me.
Help me not to judge others . . .
Until both sides of the story, I see.
Fill my heart, with Your precious love,
And put a tender smile upon my face.
Help me Lord, to spread Your word,
Until all of Your plan is in place.
Father, help me to be loving and kind,
Just the same as Jesus, would be.
Sweet Holy Spirit, please show me . . .
The meaning of God's word . . .
And please, Dear God . . . .
Let others see Jesus in me.

Some People I Remember

As I went on a journey, in my mind today.
I remembered the people, I met, along the way.
First, I thought of Chin. He really was a cut above,
Not a Christian at first, until he heard of Jesus and His love.
Yes, Chin soon became . . . quite the Christian fellow.
And it never really mattered that . . . his skin was yellow.
Then there was Mike . . . always spoiling for a fight.
Then, he met Jesus . . . now, he's such a delight.
He still has a bit of a temper, when someone's not doing right,
Still, he's a growing Christian . . . Oh, and his skin is white.
Another man soon came to mind, I grew to know him well.
He was doing "pot" and drinking, he was on the road to hell.
Then he accepted Jesus, this man that . . . . I'll call Fred.
Now, he's Heaven bound, Guess what? His skin is red.
Next comes to mind, a lady . . .
She had furs and jewels and she was well pearled.
She sang pretty songs, but they were all . . . of the world.
One night, she met Jesus, now she's on the right track.
Singing songs for Jesus now, she says, she'll never go back.
This lovely famous lady . . . her name was Roberta Flack . . .
A very special lady . . . oh yes, . . . her skin was black.
The point of the story, is this my friend . . .
It matters not, about the color of your skin.
But do you know Jesus? Do you hold Him close within?
Now I must bring this poem to an end . . .
But first . . . .
Won't you ask Jesus into your heart, right now, my friend?
God sent His Son to die for sin . . . for you and for me too!
Won't you come? He's watching . . . .
And waiting . . . right now . . . . for you!

Reach Out With Loving Arms

He reaches out with loving arms, to draw us in.
His precious Son died, to cleanse us from sin.
He reaches out with loving arms, can't you feel His touch?
Can't you feel His hand on you? He loves you very much.

He reaches out with loving arms, He gives us each a choice.
Don't you hear Him calling? Can't you hear His voice?
He reaches out with loving arms, calling from afar.
"I love you child, come to me, come, just as you are!"

He reaches out with loving arms,
To ease your care and relieve your strife.
Will you let God guide you?
Let Him have your life?
As He reaches out with loving arms,
To take away your sin,
Will you give your all to Him?
Open you heart and take Him in?
Reach out to Him with loving arms,
And don't just give Him "some."
With loving arms, reach out to Him,
When He bids you "Come!"

From The Heart Of A Child

I'm about to tell you of a situation that's bad.
It's about a child and his Mom and Dad.
The parents were both working to pay the bills,
That mounted up, like insurmountable hills.
For me there was school and what friends, I had.
But there just wasn't time, for me and my Dad.
He was too tired to play and Mom was too!
When they'd feel guilty, it was, "A new toy for you."
They went out and drank, on Friday and Saturday night.
I'd stay home and worry . . .
Whether they'd come home and fight.
One day after one of their fights, I was outside . . .
Kicking a stone, feeling kinda grim,
When a friend came over and asked . . .
If I'd go to church with him.
I said I'd go, I knew it would be okay.
On Sundays, I was always in Mom and Dad's way.
They'd be nursing a hangover or holding their head.
I'd have to be quiet, or go to bed.
So, I went to church, with that friend of mine.
I learned a lot in a very short time.

I came to know Jesus and took Him in my heart.
In my life, He became an important part.
As I learned to pray, each and every day,
I'd talk to my parents, trying to tell them of God's way.
Then as I left for church, one Sunday morning,
I had a funny feeling, a kind of a warning.
I had asked them to go to church with me.
But they said "No, Dad's boss was having them over for
Dinner and drinks." That's where they'd be.
I went on to church and back home.
I waited and worried about what they said.
Then an officer came to the door.
He told me, Mom and Dad, were dead!
I had tried to tell them, with all my might.
But the devil and his bottle, won that fight.
So parents, now, I'm asking you . . .
Do you go to church with your children, when they ask you to?
We all lost a lot that day, things we never had.
They died not knowing Jesus,
And the Eternal Life, they could have had.
Now, I'll never see them in Heaven.
I truly lost . . . . I lost my Mom and Dad.

Ode To A Prisoner

Where I am today . . . is not where I planned to be.
I had great plans for my life, you see.
I wanted a car . . . a home . . . and . . . a family.
I even dreamed . . . . of winning . . . . the lottery.
Back then, I really though, I was having fun.
Now . . . I'm ashamed . . . . of the things, I've done.
It seemed like things were going real good.
But all along, I knew . . . I wasn't living like I should.
In fact . . . the things I did . . . . were pretty bad.
See, I thought . . . I needed this "Stuff" to make me feel glad.
Then one day, the bottom fell out . . . everything went wrong.
I found out, the long arm of the law . . . is very strong.
Yea, I got caught . . . with egg on my face . .
Bound hand and foot, ... I was brought to this place.
I got here . . . scared . . . sad . . . and angry, my future looked dim.
One day, a brother asked, if I'd go to church with him . . .
I said, "No" . . . . I didn't want to go.
Well, he kept on asking . . . and I kept saying, "no."
Then one day he caught me . . . when I had the blues . . . .
So, I said I'd go . . . . I had nothing to lose.
The uplifting feeling, I got that day . . . .
It lasted all week . . . . It wouldn't go away.
I went back again . . . . and again . . . . and again.

I felt a strong kinship, with my fellow man.
The singers were good and I'd sing along
Then I joined these brothers . . . In a song.
The message in their song was loud and strong.
And the preacher was preaching . . . about what I did wrong.
When he gave the invitation, my future, no longer looked dim
Because I stepped forward . . . and prayed . . . and I received Him.
Now, I'm really glad . . . they let me take part . . .
And my gift to God . . . is the song in my heart.
We love to go to our little church here . . . .
To sing praises to our Lord.
We're also thankful . . . for all the people . . .
Who come to share . . . . God's Holy word.
When I leave here and I'm once again free . . .
I will spread His word . . . and what He's done for me.
But here's a secret . . . between you and me . . . .
Because of Jesus' love . . . . I'm already free!
Praise the Lord!!! I'm free!!!

A Church I Dreamed Of

I dreamed of a church, where I once took part,
Where sinners repented . . .
And asked Jesus, into their heart.
Or re-committed their lives . . .
And made a new start.
Broken hearts were mended,
Jesus dried their tears.
Just a little talk with Jesus
Allayed their deepest fears.
Slowly things began to change,
It all got turned around.
The tears for the lost . . . they stopped.
The smiles . . . . turned upside down.
Songs were sung without feeling . . .
Where is God's Holy Ground?
The same prayers, said the same way, every day.
Sincerity . . . was hard to be found.
God please, revive this church, . . .
The one I dreamed of . . . .
Fill it with Kindness . . .
But most of all, Lord . . .
Fill it to overflowing . . .
With Your precious love.

Your Best Friend

He listens to your troubles,
When it seems like no one else will.
He'll dry your tears, with compassion . . .
Your troubled heart, will be still.

When things seem bleak and helpless
When no one seems to care
Lift your heart to Jesus . . .
Go to Him, in prayer.

He listens to you, with love,
As He reaches out to you . . . from above.
Yes, Jesus, listens to you . . . for hours on end.
He is really and truly . . .
Your best friend.

Beggars

We are beggars, you and I,
Fighting to live, unwilling to die.
You say that you're hungry?
Well, I once was too!
Do you thirst, my friend?
Is your soul dry, within you?
I was so hungry . . . I'd sit and cry.
Though my clothes were not torn and tattered,
Still, I needed to find . . . something . . . that mattered.
I had my loved ones, but that still wasn't enough.
I had to keep searching, sometimes . . . it was tough.
Then one day, I gave up the struggle . . . I gave up the fight.
Jesus forgave me and I saw the light.
No more struggle and no more strife,
Because I've found . . . the Bread of Life.
Now, I'm so rich . . . I have everything!
I'm no longer a beggar . . . I'm telling you true.
I'm a child of the King . . . Now, how about you?
Thank You, Jesus.

One Christmas Morn

When it was within . . . . God's Master plan
He sent His Son . . . to come to Earth . . . to live and die, for man.
He chose Mary and Joseph . . . to guide His Only Son.
But what woman would bear Him? Mary, was the "only one."
Mary and Joseph, were told . . . they'd be parents to a son,
That's what God had said.
They listened and obeyed . . . and they were wed.
When it was near her time . . . and they had traveled far . . .
With no place to go to bed . . .
They had to go to Bethlehem to be counted.
The king, was counting, every head.
Now, when they had been counted . . . and all was done . . .
Mary told Joseph to "Hurry , , , The time had come."
The hotels were all full and so was the Inn.
So they went to a stable . . . to give birth to Him.
It was a cold winter night, when the tiny babe was born.
Wrapped in swaddling clothes, ... there He lay.
The Savior of the world . . . . asleep on the hay.
A certain star stood out and shone its brightest light.
And in the night, so dark and still . . .
An angels' voice was heard, out on a hill.
The shepherds heard it and knelt in prayer . . .
Knowing, their Savior, was born . . . right there.
The wise men brought gifts, as we are told . . .
Of frankincense, and myrrh . . . . and gold.
When they saw Jesus, . . . their praises did ring,
And the gifts they had brought . . . befitted a King.
This all happened . . . many years ago.
That was the very first Christmas Morn.
It was the day . . . that . . . Jesus Christ . . .
Our Lord and Savior . . . . was born!!!

Christmas Time

Christmas time, is almost here.
A time of loving and giving and Christmas cheer.
Plans for Christmas dinner and all who will come.
There are gifts to be bought and baking to be done . . .
Oh, the wrappings, the decorations, the beautiful lights!
Put them altogether . . . what memorable sights.
At church, there's the cantata, to give the spirit a lift.
And the smiles of the children . . . awaiting their gift.
Outside we see the fresh fallen snow.
The full moon, in the sky . . . just adds to the glow.
I heard someone say, "It's gotten too commercial for me!"
Allow me to tell you, the things that I see.

I see the tree, reminding me, that the cross of Jesus, was made from a tree.
The lights, tell me, He was and is, the light of the world, for you and me.
The star? It led the wise men, to where the Christ child lay.
The King of the world . . . asleep on the hay.
The gifts, beneath the tree, that brings a smile to each face,
Should remind us of the gifts, the Magi brought to that place.
Little angels, float all around that tree . . .
Still proclaiming a message . . . to you and me.
"Fear not . . . You are in no danger . . .
For unto you, is born a Savior, in Bethlehem . . .
Wrapped in Swaddling clothes . . . lying in a manger."
A host of Angels, appeared that night.
For a moment, they gave the shepherds, a fright.
Their fear, didn't last, so very long.
Because these lovely angels, burst into song . . . .
Saying, "Glory to God in the highest . . .
Peace in Earth, good will to man."
So as you sing your Christmas carols . . .
Remember, if you can . . . .
Lift your voice to Heaven, sing to God above.
Thank Him for His gift to you . . . .
The gift of . . . Jesus . . . and His love.
Have a Blessed Christmas!

What Do You Want For Christmas?

My love asked me . . .
"What do you want for Christmas?"
He said it with love and concern in his voice.
"Money is no object . . . so think hard . . .
And make your choice.
I thought about it for days . . .
Hmmm . . . What would I choose?
I could have anything at all?
Why . . . I couldn't lose.
A new carpet? A couch and maybe a ring?
How about a new house?
He had said . . . Anything!
Then in the stillness of the night . . . I began to listen to my heart.
All those things, I had thought of . . .
Could break . . . rot . . . or fall apart.
What I really wanted, would be from God above.
A heart full of tenderness, kindness, peace and love.
He said, I could have all of that . . . and more.
If I'd open my heart's door and turn from sin.
So I opened the door and He entered in.
I got what I wanted for Christmas, from God above.
A heart full of Jesus and wrapped in His love.
Thank You, Jesus

What Does Christmas Mean To Me?

What does Christmas mean to me?
Is it gifts and tinsel . . .
And a Christmas tree?
No, it's a tiny baby, sent from God above . . .
And He brought to Earth, the gift, of love.
He shared that love so grand and free.
As a man . . . He gave His life . . . for you and me.
So you can keep the gifts . . .
The holly, the tinsel . . .
And the Christmas tree.
I'll still have the love of Jesus . . .
That's what Christmas means to me.

The Christmas Tree

The
Tree itself
Should remind us
Of the tree our Lord
Was crucified on. The lights
Tell us that Jesus, was, is and
Always will be, The light of the world.
The tinsel, shining and streaming down,
Shows us but a faint glimmer, of the love
of God, that streams down to us, at all times.
The star at the top of the tree, represents the
Star of Bethlehem that shone so brightly, the night
that Jesus was born. It shone so bright, it led the wise
men to where Jesus lay in a manger, a new born babe,
from God. The gifts beneath the tree, should remind
us of the gifts the wise men brought from afar, to honor
Jesus, the Savior of the world. The gifts they brought
were things that would honor, a king, Our King! They also
represented the ultimate gift. The gift that Jesus offers
to all of us. Eternal Life! He paid a high price for that
gift. He gave His life, that we might live. If only we reach
out and accept that gift.
Thank You
Jesus!
Merry Christmas

A New Year's Prayer

Another year is ending, quickly coming to a close.
I want to thank You Father,
For taking me down the paths, You chose.
The road wasn't always smooth
And a lot of times it went up hill.
But You always cleared the way for me,
As long as I stayed in Your will.
Sometimes, I faltered, as I walked along life's way.
Yet, You were there to give me Your strength,
To see me through each day.
When I was ill, Your healing power came through.
Oh, my God, my Father, how I love You.
So, as this year closes and another year begins . . .
Father, please forgive me, of my daily sins.
Let me walk bravely, on that rough and uphill road.
Let me be aware of Your strength,
That's always there to lighten my load.
When I'm in doubt, Father, calm my fears,
And if I should cry, please kiss away my tears.
If I falter, as I walk along life's way,
Dear God, give me strength,
To see me through each day.
As this night and this year ends . . .
And my heart is still,
My prayer for each day of the new year,
Is to walk steadfastly, in Your will.
Amen

Promised Land

When I feel the darkness, I can see the fire.
Lead me God, with Your cloud today.
Your command, is my heart's desire.
You led Your children out of Egypt,
Right through the Red Sea, they walked on dry land.
They were Your "peculiar" people,
So You led them with Your mighty hand.
You chose Moses to lead them, to walk Your way.
You gave them a cloud to follow, all through the day.
You planned ahead, with Your wise insight,
And gave them a fire to guide them by night.
When they were hungry, they did murmur and complain.
Still, You forgave them and fed them, again and again.
You led them out of Egypt, through the desert,
Through the Red Sea, to dry land.
Now, I pray dear Lord, lead me out of the chains of bondage,
Through the desert of trials, by Your mighty hand.
Help me show others, Your infinite love,
Until You take me to Your Promised Land . . .
To my Heavenly home, above.

When I Leave This World

When I leave this world, I won't go alone.
An angel will come, to take me home.
I'll be led, into the light, to Heaven's gate.
Then, I'll see Jesus, for this . . . I wait.
My knees shall bend, as I bow, when we meet.
I will humbly place a kiss, on my Jesus' feet.
The book will be checked, then I can go in,
Because Jesus has forgiven my sin.
Streets of transparent gold, will be a treat,
I'll giggle, if I can slide on them, in my stocking feet.
I'll see my loved ones, who have gone on before.
They'll be watching for me . . .
To come through Heaven's door . . .
We'll sing and praise Jesus and dance with glee,
Thanking Jesus . . . . for saving me.
There will be no sickness, no disappointment,
No tears or sorrow, in Heaven above.
The only thing there, will be the purest of love.
But . . . before I go . . . there's one thing, I want you to know.
When I leave this world, I won't go alone.
An angel will come . . . . to take me home.

Genesis One

Once upon a nothing,
God reached out His mighty hand.
He rolled nothing into something and He called it Earth.
It was God's Mighty land.
Then He divided this nothing, into something devine . . .
Into seas and rivers and air and dry land.
Everything was clean and beautiful,
And God said, "That's fine!"
God said, "This Earth, needs light."
And there was light, God called it "Day."
Then God said, "We need some darkness,
To make things balance right."
So, there was darkness, God called it "Night."
Into the water, the fishes went,
And into the air, the birds were sent.
On the land, God put animals, of every kind.
Then God created man, with a body, a soul and a mind.
God called the man Adam, of the Earth, he came.
Then God told him to rule over the animals,
And give each one a name.
God put Adam, in the garden of Eden.
There, he could eat of all but one tree.
He was happy for all of these things, But

He was the only man and poor Adam, was lonely.
Now, God could see loneliness in Adam's life.
He put Adam to sleep, took one of his ribs . . .
And from that, He made for Adam, a wife.
Then He blessed them. He said,
"Be fruitful and multiply and fill the Earth!
Subdue it . . . for all you're worth.
I give you dominion over the fish and the fowl,
And all that moves upon the Earth.
"Also, I've given you herb bearing seed and
Every tree, with fruit bearing seed,
So you'll have food, wherever you go . . .
And to the beast of the Earth and the fowl of the air,
To everything that creepeth on Earth,
I've given herbs for food" . . . and it was so!
God saw everything that He made and it was very good.
And the evening and the morning, were the sixth day, . . .
From where, He stood.

Exodus Chapter 1

When Jacob came into Egypt, He brought his family too.
His son Joseph, was Pharoh's top officer,
Joseph told Jacob, what to do.
Then Joseph and Jacob died.
And the rest of that generation that came.
But the children of Israel were fruitful,
And they multiplied, just the same.
They were mighty, in all of Egypt,
They truly, filled the land.
There arose a new king in Egypt.
He was very mean and cruel.
He didn't have the experience . . .
He didn't know Joseph's rule. He told the Egyptians,
That the Israelites, they must subdue.
He set task masters over them.
The Pharoh's bidding, they must do.
But the more the Egyptians afflicted them . . .
The more they grew and grew. The Israelites lives were bitter,
With hard work in mortar and in brick.
Pharoh ordered, boy babies to die . . .
But the midwives, knew a trick.
They feared Almighty God,
And they saved each baby boy's life.
When Pharoh asked, "Why?" they said . . .
Israeli women, deliver faster than an Egyptian wife.
So Pharoh's order to his people was . . .
That each baby boy, born on Egyptian ground . . .
Must be cast into the river . . .
Until the baby boy, was drowned.

Exodus Chapter II, Part I

A Levite man married a Levite woman, Miriam, was her name.
First they had a daughter, a good girl, without shame.
Miriam was with child again, it was a boy,
When the birthing time came.
She hid this boy baby for three months,
With a great deal of care.
Then she knew, she must do something,
With her baby boy, so fair.
She made him an ark of bulrushes . . .
Covered with slime and pitch.
She put the baby in the ark and put both in the reeds, . . .
In a river . . . not a ditch.
His sister watched, to make sure he'd be okay.
Pharoh's daughter, found the baby . . .
The very next day.
She looked at him and cried,
And wanted him for her own.
But she knew nothing about babies.
She couldn't take care of him, alone.
The baby's sister, ran up to say . . .
She knew of a nurse, who would take care of the baby boy.
It was agreed! She ran home to get her mother,
Whose heart was filled with joy.
She had her baby back and Pharoh's daughter paid her too!
Time did pass, the baby became a child . . .
Then a boy . . . how rapidly, he grew.
He was returned to the palace, to the arms of Pharoh's daughter.
He became her son, She named him Moses,
Because she drew him out of the water.

Exodus Chapter II, Part II

When Moses was all grown, he went to see the work,
That his brethren, had to do.
See. Moses was an Israelite, it was something he always knew.
An Egyptian was beating a Hebrew brother,
Moses looked around and saw no other . . . .
So he hit the Egyptian and killed him, with his own hand.
Then he dug a hole and buried the Egyptian, in the sand.
The second day, he saw two brothers in a fight,
He asked them, "What's the fuss?"
One of them asked him,
"Who made you a prince and a judge, over us?"
Are you going to kill me,
Like you did the Egyptian, yesterday?"
Moses feared and said, "My sin is known,
I'd better run away."
When Pharoh heard about it . . .
He wanted to kill Moses . . . that very day.
But Moses fled to Midian, a town, not far away.
When he got there, he was thirsty,
And he sat down by a well.
He decided, Midian, was the place,
Where he wanted to dwell.
Seven daughters of the Midian Priest,
Came to the well that day.
They came for water for themselves
And their father's sheep.

But other shepherds came and drove the girls away.
But Moses stood up and helped them,
That day . . . they beat the clock.
They went home and told their father . . .
That Moses, drew water for them . . .
And he also watered the flock.
He told them to go get Moses,
And feed him a meal, for helping with the water.
Moses decided to live with the man.
The man gave Moses, Zipporah, his daughter.
They were blessed with a child, Gershom, was his name.
For Moses said, "I've been a stranger, in a strange land,
Much different than Egypt, from whence I came.

Commit

(This was written for an inmate when we were in prison ministry)

I once had a woman that loved me.
We lived together for a long, long while.
She loved me so much, she even bore me a child.
But, our life together . . . was pretty wild.
She began to go to church, then, she got "Saved."
Then. She said we were "living in sin."
She said, I needed to change. I said, "Where do I begin?"
She said, we needed to get married. I said. "No, that was it."
She took the baby and left, just because I wouldn't "Commit."
She wanted me to give up drinking, drugs and all my "Nights out."
All this religious stuff, had warped her mind . . . no doubt!
She even wanted me to give up . . . . my best friend!
I thought it would wear off and she'd come back, in the end.
But there was no way, I was going to change . . .
Not even a little bit!
Knowing how much I liked all these things . . .
Why would she think . . . I'd ever quit?
All of this happened because of one word . . . . "Commit."
I loved her and I missed her, . . .
So I started to go to church too.
I only went to please her. I wasn't going to change . . . mind you.
The preacher's words . . . they struck my heart . . .
Then, as my sins were revealed . . . it tore me apart.
One night . . . I turned it over to Jesus.
I was finally ready, to give it all up and quit.
Since then, my Lord, has taught me . . .
What it means to . . . . Commit.

Here I Go

Well, it's Revival time again . . . and I guess you know . . .
The wife and kids have been at me.
They're tryin' to get me to go.
Just listen to 'em . . . just a pesterin' me.
And there's that special, tonight, on T.V.
"There'll be special singin' . . . better'n that show."
"Okay . . . Okay . . . . Here I go."
Boy, I can't think of a good excuse, like I usually do.
Ahah!!! I'm almost dressed now . . .
Hon? . . . I can't find my left shoe!
You and the kids, just go on without me . . .
I'll just watch that show . . . on T.V.
Oh, you found my shoe? Well . . . whatta ya' k now!
Ah well . . . . Here I go.
Since they started going to church and got religion . . .
They just keep askin' me . . .
Well, I went with them about a month ago . . .
Or was it two or three?
Just listen now . . . Are you ready? Are you ready?
Man . . . I'd like to say . . . "No."
Yeah . . . Yeah . . . . I'm comin' . . . Here I go!
Well, we're on our way . . . just one more red light.
Oh well, guess it won't hurt me . . . .
To miss T.V. tonight.
Wow, look at all those cars! There's quite a few!
That's my neighbor, in front of me . . .

And my boss is here too!
Well, I'll put on a smile, shake hands with the preacher
And put on a good show.
Almost there now . . . . Here I go!
I know some of these people . . . in fact, quite a few!
There's Frank and his family and Sam's over there too!
I can see about everyone from here.
I'm sure glad we sat in this back pew.
Say those singers are good . . . maybe I was wrong.
Let's see now . . . I've heard that song.
It's their version of "The Lord's Prayer . . . and now . . .
"Will my mother know me, over there?"
There's one more song and then they're done.
It's a new one to me . . . it's called . . . "I'm The One."
Now what's the preachin' gonna be?
Whoa . . . sounds like he's talkin' just to me . . .
About makin' excuses . . . why I can't come . . .
Now, he's even namin' some.
Sure, I got saved . . . when I was thirteen.
But I kinda slipped away . . . if you know what I mean
Sure, I know, I should come back . . . I know . . . I know!
But that aisle looks sooo long . . . well, here I go!
Dear God . . . I am sorry . . . I stayed away so long.
Please forgive me . . . for doing You wrong.
From now on . . . I want to live for You . . . each day . . .
And let everything I say and do . . . be Your way.
Lord, I'm not puttin' on a show and this is no "sham."
Heavenly Father, if You can use me . . . Here I am!

Was It Worth It After All?

When I was a child and did something that wasn't right . . .
Mom would spank me and put me to bed . . .
And it wasn't even night!
Then. I'd say I was sorry . . . as I stood there in the hall.
Mom'd hug and kiss me and say, "Was it worth it after all?"
Then I got into my teenage years . . .
And rebellion, quickly replaced my fears.
By then, I knew what was right from wrong . . .
But I'd do wrong anyway . . . I was so headstrong.
My parents would yell at me . . . that didn't matter at all.
Then came the punishment . . . and I'd wonder . . . .
"Was it worth it after all?"
I worked hard at home . . . but not in school.
I didn't want to be serious . . . so I acted like a fool.
I was too tired to study, when I came in from my work . . .
So, I'd go to bed . . . and my studies . . . I'd shirk.
Report Card!!! Oooo . . . I'd hear Dad's angry call.
"You're grounded! You and your silliness!!!
Now, was it worth it after all?"
Too soon, I got married . . .
Just to get away from home.
But crying babies, getting meals, plus house work . . .
It just bored me to the bone.
The boy . . . he really wasn't very nice . . .
We were both far too young.
But that's another sad song, that needn't be sung.
Cheating and name calling and beatings and all . . .
I thought . . . "Why did I leave home?
Was it worth it after all?"

That marriage ended, but life went on . . .
It went from bad to worse.
Bad things kept happening in my life . . .
I thought I was under some curse.
I went to bars . . . I drank and danced . . .
You likely know the scene.
I played the part, I walked the walk and talked the talk . . . .
Well, ... you know what I mean.
Then I met a different man, gentle and very tall.
He began to teach me that my "Lifestyle"
Wasn't worth it, after all.
I married that man and we went to church . . . .
Each Sunday morning and night.
Still I refused to accept Jesus . . .
I held back, with all my might.
Why, I'd have to give up drinkin' and dancin' . . .
And what did Christians do for fun?
Then one day, I asked Jesus, into my heart.
My victory . . . was won!
I turned my life, over to Him . . . heart and soul and all.
Now, I know true peace and love . . .
And it was worth it after all.
Have you accepted Jesus? Have you given Him your life?
If you do, He'll forgive your sin . . .
And end the pain and strife.
You'll be a brand new creature . . . a whole new you!
You'll have no fear of satan or hell . . .
Cause, you'll go to Heaven too!
Because of your sin, they took Jesus up a hill . . .
And nailed Him, to a tree so tall.
Won't you ask Jesus into your heart . . . right now? . . .
And make it worth it after all!!!

Hello Jesus, Come On In

I hear You knockin' Jesus, Won't You please come in?
You know, I've been thinkin' Jesus . . .
All about this thing called sin.
I need You Jesus . . . there is no doubt!
These are the sins, I've had to think about.
All those times, I got too drunk to drive . . . ?
I've got you to thank, that I'm still alive.
And those drugs I took, just to keep me "high?"
Lord, it's a miracle that I didn't die.
Then I stole things, for the drugs I couldn't buy.
When someone would ask, "Did you steal that?"
I'd just stand right there and lie.
I told my wife and kids, . . . "I'll change . . .
And I won't do those things anymore."
But then, I'd bottom out and . . .
Know, I'd have to "score."
Then my wife took the kids and left me.
Lord, I was so high . . . I didn't even care.
She took the kids, the clothes and the furniture.
I was left with a house that was bare.
What was a home and a family . . . just wasn't anymore.
I screamed and yelled and cursed,
As I defiantly, slammed the door.
I went to live with my brother and his wife,
But my lifestyle, they began to condemn.
We had a fight about money, so, I moved away from them.
So, I turned completely to these "friends" of mine.
I went deeper and deeper, into a life of crime.

One night, I robbed a store and as I turned around . . .
Someone yelled, I heard a shot, then, I hit the ground.
I opened my eyes to look around the place.
What I saw was an officer, with his gun in my face.
I was sentenced, for that night of crime.
I admit. I was guilty, so I'm serving my time.
Since I got here, I've gone to church . . . a time or two.
Where I've learned about love and sin and . . . about You.
Sweet gentle Jesus, I am coming to You now.
I want to be saved, but I'm not sure how.
Well dear Jesus, I guess I'll just begin.
Lord, up until today, I've lived a life of sin.
I'm so sorry Jesus, please forgive me, I pray.
I want to turn away from sin and turn to You today.
I know You died upon that tree . . .
If for no one else, You did it Lord, for me.
You rose to Heaven, to sit at the Father's right hand.
I know now, Jesus, when I die . . .
I want to go to that sweet Beulah land.

I'm turning my life over to You,
Please give me power over sin.
I've opened my heart's door, for You to come in.
I'll try to be faithful, as I can be.
And Thank You, Jesus . . . .
For saving a sinner, like me.

A Loving Farewell

Before I go to sleep tonight,
There's something I must say.
I've loved you all so very much,
But soon now, I must go away.
That "Distant Land" is calling me,
To a mansion, in the sky.
But we'll soon be together again,
My dear ones, don't you cry.
Think of all the good times we've all had,
And how I scolded, when you were bad.
Those "Honey Do" weekends,
When nothing got done . . . but shopping,
And dinner, after church and a little fun . . . .
We didn't have much money.
But we had more than most folks do.
We had God in our hearts, to guide us,
And our love for each other too!
Don't forget the good things and don't remember the bad.
Just remember God's love, is the best thing we ever had.
Bundle up when it's cold, remember to rest in the heat.
Wash your neck and ears and don't forget, your feet.
Take your pills, the way you should
And try real hard, to be very good.
When I go to the Promised Land,
I'll place you all in God's Loving Hand.
Love, Momma

Dearly Beloved

Dearly Beloved,
Oh, the glory I see before me,
His promise, He is keeping.
I can see the gates of Heaven now,
Rejoice, my loves, stop weeping.

There is no pain, no tears, no sorrow.
There is no yesterday and no tomorrow.
There is brightness and beauty . . . .
As the Bible, foretold.
I'm walking now, on the streets of gold.

He prepared for me a mansion,
Just the way He said He would.
You can't imagine the beauty here,
No one ever could!

Today, I met Joseph, Isaac, Mark and John!
The list is endless, it goes on and on.
When I arrived, I was greeted by saints,
And by angels alike.
I also talked with Grandma and Grandpa . . .
And cousin Mike.

My Beloved ones, I must go now.
There are so many things to do.
So weep no more loves, just Rejoice!
I'm here in Heaven . . . .
Watching and waitng, for you.

Departed

A dear one has departed,
From this Earth, they have gone.
The fears . . . . the pain . . . the tears,
Have been erased.
The victory, has been won.
No more struggle . . .
With the things of this Earth.
The cares of this world . . .
Are no longer of worth.
The body, once wracked with pain,
Is now complete and free,
Walking the streets of Heaven . . .
Praising God and waiting . . . .
Waiting for you and me.
But are you sure you will go . . .
To meet Jesus and your loved one, face to face?
Or are you still clinging to the world . . . and satan?
Will you go to the other place?
If you're not right with God . . .
Please, don't wait.
Turn to Him now . . . before it's too late!
Take Him into your heart . . .
And through His saving Grace . . .
You'll be assured . . . You'll meet your loved one . . .
In that greater place.

Soon

My eyes will soon see Jesus,
He is the Savior of my soul.
When we meet, I'll fall on my knees,
And He will touch and make me whole.
There will be no more heartache., no more pain.
No tears of sadness, will ever flow again.
I'll have no cares of yesterday,
No thoughts about tomorrow,
Mysteries in my life, I will be shown.
Answers to my questions, will be known.
He will take me by the hand . . . .
Together, we will cross over to the Promised Land.
I'll see loved ones souls,
Who have gone on before me.
We will sing His praises and dance with glee.
Everything there will be sweet and true.
I'll smile when I hear Him say, . . .
"Come now, My child, I love you!"
Oh, I want to see Jesus, face to face,
To feel His love and be filled with His grace.
Until then, there are things on Earth, for me to do,
To tell others of Jesus' love and that
He wants to save them too.
I want to introduce you to Jesus . . .
That is my goal.
My eyes will soon see Jesus,
He is the Savior of my soul.
Now, my friend, you know what you must do.
Ask Jesus, into your heart.
This is His message, through me . . .
To you.

CPSIA information can be obtained
at www.ICGtesting.com
Printed in the USA
FFOW01n0755120517
35477FF